Go Global!

Launching an International
Career Here or Abroad

Stacie Nevadomski Berdan

SNB Media LLC

Designed by Jessica Vernick

ISBN: 978-0-9839439-1-4, paperback
ISBN: 978-0-9839439-0-7, eBook

This book is dedicated to my husband, Mike:

Thank you for making my life infinitely richer
by sharing so many global adventures with me.

Acknowledgments

Many thanks to my friends and colleagues who shared their experiences with me and spent time discussing the merits of this book and how best to advise today's new globetrotters. Thanks to the many professors and students who took the time to give me feedback on the topics most important to you.

Particular thanks to those who contributed their stories and patiently waited for the arrival of this book: Rosary Abot, Marty Abbott, George Birman, Terrence Brake, Christy Brown, Curtis S. Chin, Matt Conway, Beth Cubanski, Constance deNazelle, Ben Farkas, Robert Fried, Allison Frick, Diane Gulyas, Andrew Howe, Caitlin Kappel, Carleen Kerttula, Sharon Knight, Elizabeth Knup, Kelly Loughlin, Elizabeth Marshman, John Miles, Nicholas Musy, Lauren Nelson, Ben Paulker, Ramiro Prudencio, Liesl Riddle, Gus Tate, Kate Triggs, Hailey Weiss, Perry Yeatman and Michael Zhu.

Special thanks to my illustrative friends: my sister, Ellen Nevadomski, and friend, Philip Kleimenhagen, who helped me with charts, graphs and multi-media components; Andy Nebel and Michael Huffer who produced the Go Global! video; and to Jessica Vernick for creating the book cover.

Special thanks to those who read the final manuscript: Morgan Abate, my niece, guest- and ghost-blogger and a budding writer; Beth Cubanski, a contributor and student at the American University pursuing pre-med and Spanish; and Laura Cubanski, friend, excellent editor and fellow parent trying to raise globally-aware children.

Special thanks to three friends and former colleagues: Rebecca Weiner, who authored the chapter on China and whose superb writing skills smoothed the kinks out making the book a better read. Curtis S. Chin, former US Ambassador, whose thoughtful and substantive comments enriched the book and whose wise counsel kept me focused on the end result. Barbara Levy, fellow global traveler, whose creative inspiration enabled me to think beyond the boundaries and whose listening skills got me through the final production of this book.

Finally, thank you to my family for your love, support and understanding. It means so much to me.

Contents

About the Author

I wrote my first book *Get Ahead By Going Abroad: A Woman's Guide to Fast-Track Career Success* (co-authored with C. Perry Yeatman and published by HarperCollins in 2007) after spending almost 20 years in the corporate world.

I have spent most of my career as a marketing communications strategist. I took a risk and moved to Washington, D.C., after grad school without a job because I loved politics and the buzz of the capital. I landed a great job with Burson-Marsteller, the largest global public relations agency. I rose from an entry-level assistant account executive to global account managing director. After five years working toward and hoping for an international assignment, I was transferred to Hong Kong, one of my favorite cities in the world, where I grew both personally and professionally. I made some of my closest friends there. I attribute a great deal of my fast-track success to my ability to differentiate and distinguish myself upon my return to Washington, D.C., where I tripled my salary and jumped from vice-president to global account managing director – despite taking 6 months maternity leave. After years at B-M, I took a job at Unilever, a global consumer products company. While there I led the communications teams responsible for strategy and execution of the new global brand and an $11 billion integration of multiple business units into one operating unit.

I have served as coach, counselor, strategist and adviser to CEOs, politicians, senior executives and students around the world, and my cross-cultural consulting experience enables me to work with a diverse mixture of professionals across industry, seniority level, nationality and gender. I have traveled to and worked in more than 50 countries, and I have been responsible for global, cross-cultural teams of professionals in 25 markets.

Today I write and speak about current trends in the global workforce, offering advice to students and professionals, career counselors and human resource leaders. You'll find me as an international career expert blogging on the Huffington Post, tweeting about all things global, and providing advice via interviews and articles in news outlets. To check out my recent posts, go to **www.stacieberdan.com**, and while you're there, sign up to receive Go Global! updates. My ongoing experience informs this book so that you, too, can be better prepared to GO GLOBAL!

Introduction to Go Global!

Welcome to *Go Global! Launching an International Career Here or Abroad.*
I'm happy that you're here because it means you are serious about your
career in this brave new international age. Whether you're a high
school student, undergrad or grad student, or you already have your
degree, you've come to the right place to arm yourself with the most
up-to-date, strategic advice and practical tips on what it means to go
global.

The global marketplace is huge. Dynamic. And yes, it can be a bit
scary. You deal with different cultures, currencies, languages, history,
politics, religions. Global workers must cope with all these and more as
they both search for jobs and then work across borders either virtually
or physically. I'm here to help you navigate your way through the maze
of an international career.

First, let's clarify the term international career upfront. **It does not
necessarily mean moving or working abroad.** An international
career requires employees to conduct their work across national
borders or between at least two cultures within a single country. It
does not necessarily mean working and living outside your home
country. The "international" in some jobs means that you work with
global clients, customers or people; you will be based in your home
country and may not even have to travel overseas. Some international
jobs require frequent global travel and oversight. Others still offer a
mix of assignments at home and abroad. All these jobs require
international workers with skills relevant to cross-cultural, cross-border
success, and top-notch technical knowledge.

To that most worthy end, this book will help you navigate the steps
to launching an international career.

About this Book

You don't have to read this book from beginning to end, but you might want to – and it's not too long. *Go Global! Launching an International Career Here or Abroad* follows a progression that provides answers to the questions you're facing as you decide how to launch an international career.

I begin with an overview of why you need to think about globalization, provide details on how you can acquire and market relevant international qualifications, and then move into specific strategic planning advice to launch your international career. I conclude with advice on how to make the move, first generally, and then very specifically with an eye on China – one of the hottest job markets in the world and one of the most important for the future – as the target in the final chapter.

Each chapter stands alone and will serve as a go-to resource throughout your ongoing journey. Sprinkled throughout the book are anecdotes, stories and tips – real-life examples from students through to seasoned experts – that make the advice come alive with relevance. Some of these stories are actually multi-media and you'll need to be able to connect to watch them. Although not many, you won't want to miss them, so be sure to check them out; they're highlighted in the text.

The best part about this book? I offer you the opportunity to ask me additional questions, provide feedback, make requests for more content and even offer additional advice to fellow readers, directly via email to me (Stacie@stacieberdan.com). I will then share this additional content and create an ongoing dialogue among like-minded global citizens on my website, to enrich the *Go Global!* experience.

About the Contributors

Sprinkled throughout the book are anecdotes, stories and tips that enhance the practical advice of *Go Global!* So as not to interrupt the flow of the text with introductions throughout, I've listed all contributors here with first-person biographical snapshots.

Rosary Abot: I graduated from the University of Notre Dame with a degree in Chemical Engineering and Philosophy. My year abroad at King's College, Cambridge, allowed me to continue to study both fields and to explore the intersection of science, technology and philosophy. Over the last few years, I have had the privilege of teaching English in Mongolia, conducting soft materials research and working in industry.

Marty Abbott: I am Executive Director for the American Council on the Teaching of Foreign Languages (ACTFL). Our organization promotes language learning for all students at all grade levels. Our national public awareness campaign, ***Discover Languages…Discover the World!,*** serves both our membership and the general public to help spread the word! I am a former high school Spanish and Latin teacher, and Coordinator of the Language Programs for the Fairfax County (VA) Public Schools. I love to cook special recipes for my friends and family and travel to new places.

Jessica Austin: I'm an American who has been living in the Netherlands since 1999. I held senior management and director-level positions at prestigious corporate and academic organizations for 10 years. I am a certified coach and trainer with 17 years of US and Pan-European HR, recruitment, career education, coaching and training experience, primarily in the areas of intercultural communication skills, leadership development, professional and personal transition, and mobility and assimilation. I love the sun, the sea and rollerblading with my daughter.

Terence Brake: I'm a regional president of TMA World, a worldwide company specializing in global talent development for Fortune 500 clients. I've worked on – and with – global virtual teams for more than a decade and have written several books, including my most recent title, "Where in the World is My Team" (Wiley 2008).

Christine Brown: After a long career in language and international education as well as serving as Assistant School Superintendent for the Glastonbury (CT) Public Schools, I am trying out a new career as Deputy Director of the American International School in Santo Domingo, Dominican Republic. I have been abroad many times as an exchange student, a language educator and an educational consultant, but now I will actually be working overseas. I credit the early language learning experiences I had with the comfort level I feel both in working and living abroad and at home in diverse ethnic communities.

Curtis S. Chin: As the son of a registered nurse and a US military officer stationed to posts around the world, I spent my youth in Bangkok, Seoul, Taipei and the US states of Arizona, Maryland and Virginia. I had a 20+ year career with global communications giant Burson-Marsteller, working from Washington, D.C., Tokyo, Beijing; Hong Kong and New York HQ, as well as stopping to earn an MBA from Yale along the way. Twenty years later, I was appointed by President George W. Bush to serve as the US Ambassador to the Asian Development Bank, and was based in Manila. I currently advise a range of non-profit organizations and emerging ventures on Board development and start-up issues.

Matt Conway: I recently graduated from the University of Connecticut, majoring in Finance. During my college career, I had a number of domestic internships and one in Dublin. Before beginning my full-time position at General Electric's FMP rotation, I traveled throughout Western Europe and participated in a service trip in Peru.

Beth Cubanski: I'm currently an undergrad studying Spanish and science at American University. My goal is a career with Doctors Without Borders or some similar organization, preferably in Latin America. In an effort to further that objective, I worked as a volunteer medical interpreter at a free clinic for migrant farmworkers from Mexico over the summer. I enjoy trying new things, especially foods, vacations and seeing my sisters when I'm home from college.

Constance deNazelle: I was born in Holland and lived there for four years before moving to Singapore, where I lived for the next twelve years. I am studying Business and Public Policy at the Wharton School of Business at the University of Pennsylvania. But as I am actually French, I go back to France every summer. Last summer, I worked as an intern at a corporate law firm in Paris. As my academic and professional careers progress, I hope to be able to continue to engage my love of travel and experiencing other cultures around the world.

Ben Farkas: After college at Princeton I taught for a year in Jishou, in western Hunan Province, China, writing a blog about my experiences there and learning to like spicy food. I'm now returning to the States and enrolling at Yale Law School. I like to hike, cook and play piano.

Allison Frick: I'm currently working as a sports producer for dc.highschoolsports.net, a Gannett website based at CBS affiliate W*USA 9 in Washington, DC. While studying broadcast journalism and Spanish at the University of Maryland, I worked at the university's cable news station, had a business internship in Costa Rica, and interned at W*USA. My goal is to take the broad foundation of reporting skills I am learning and transfer them into a Spanish-speaking market.

Robert Fried: I'm the founding director of the Chinese Language Institute (CLI), an educational services organization based in southern China. While studying in Beijing during my senior year of college, I launched CLI from my dorm room and have since grown the company to include 18 employees and a newly renovated 5-story learning center. To date, we've hosted more than 100 students from all over the world, including those from Harvard, Yale, Columbia and Oxford. I'm passionate about learning, creating, designing, documenting and exploring.

Diane Gulyas: Going global at an early stage was certainly the key to my successful rise within DuPont. After ten years working for DuPont in the US, I went overseas in 1989 with high-profile stints in Switzerland and Belgium and returned four years later as Assistant to the CEO. I was then named VP and general manager for DuPont's Advanced Fiber Business. I now serve as President of Performance Polymers, and spend a good deal of my time traveling, especially in Asia and South America.

Andrew Howe: After college in the US and France, I taught for a year in a middle school in rural Hunan Province. I am now beginning a Master's program focusing on rural livelihoods and food sovereignty in Francophone Africa at the University of Oregon.

Caitlin Kappel: I'm a second-year MBA student at the NYU Stern School of Business, specializing in Finance and Financial Instruments and Markets. I hold an undergraduate degree in Chemistry, with a minor in Entrepreneurship from Johns Hopkins University. Prior to returning to grad school, I worked at Thomson Reuters in Corporate Advisory Services for four years. This summer I interned in Sales & Trading at Credit Suisse in New York City. When I'm not busy with school, I love to travel and watch any Pittsburgh sports team play.

Carleen Kerttula: I currently serve as executive director of the MBA Roundtable, an association of 160+ business schools whose mission is to advance curricular change and innovation in MBA education. My passion for global citizenry and management education comes from a 20-year career with roles as diverse as MBA program and career services director for a leading business school, collegiate instructor of French, international sales and marketing manager for a Fortune 1000 corporation, and public relations intern for a large regional French newspaper.

Sharon Knight: Two years ago, I was a Senior Vice President with one of the world's largest videogame developers, which I came by after a fabulous 2-1/2 year stint in London running European product operations for the company. My work in Europe resulted in a promotion and a transfer back to US headquarters to create a global shared service organization and to lead the company's worldwide outsourcing and offshoring operations. I held this position, traveling the world, for two years before deciding I wanted to run the show at a more entrepreneurial healthcare start-up company. My husband and I live in San Francisco; I work hard to feed our travel bug whenever I can.

Elizabeth Knup: I studied Chinese in college, and have been involved with China since the 1980s. Today I live in Beijing, where I am chief China representative for Pearson, the world-leading education company that owns Penguin Books, the *Financial Times*, and the Pearson educational resources and technology company.

Kelly Loughlin: I'm currently an HR & Recruiting Coordinator at StumbleUpon Inc. in San Francisco. American by birth, I grew up in Hong Kong, where I attended an international school and got to travel extensively, especially in Asia and Australia. I earned my B.A. in Asian

12

Studies from the University of Denver. I enjoy exploring new places, painting and running along the bay in beautiful San Francisco.

Elizabeth Marshman: A 2010 graduate of Yale, I now serve as Executive Director of ReEnvision Design, a non-profit, in addition to freelancing as an engineer in the Bay Area. At ReEnvision, I work primarily with major universities, government organizations, corporations and not-for-profit organizations in designing practical solutions for major issues surrounding poverty: e.g., medical devices for clinics without access to power or clean water, water systems that decrease infant mortality rates from 50% to less than 10%, and mobile clinics to provide medical and dental services to populations that have no other access. My vision is for engineering and design to eventually eradicate global poverty.

John C. Miles: I am a dual US/UK citizen and former singer in the New York Metro Mass Choir. I was an English major and pre-med student at Duke University, where I also earned my MBA. I spent the eight years prior to business school at Goldman Sachs, working with financial institutions in various business development and relationship management roles, with projects in Bermuda, London and Bangalore.

Nicholas Musy: I was born in Switzerland, and have travelled throughout the world. I first came to China in the early 1980s and became interested in business, starting a small sportswear manufacturing operation which grew to a chain of companies that I eventually sold. Today I consult for other start-ups via co-leading China Integrated. In my spare time, I am a distance runner and an environmental activist and have helped create an annual ultra-marathon in Mongolia that helps raise funds for Mongolia's national parks.

Lauren Nelson: I graduated from Boston University in 2009 with majors in International Relations and Political Science. As a student, I lived and studied in Peru and Ecuador, where I volunteered with local NGOs in the fields of youth mentorship and the education of indigenous populations. Since graduation, I've resided in southern China, where I first taught secondary and university level English, but now act as the educational director for an American-founded Chinese language and culture institute. I will be moving to India to take part in an NGO fellowship funded by American Jewish World Service.

Ben Paulker: I'm an undergrad and an International Marketing Major at The George Washington University in Washington, D.C. I currently work for an international marketing firm called The Noral Group. I have studied languages all of my life and continue to use these skills in order to better my understanding of the world around me. I love sports and movies along with traveling the world.

Ramiro Prudencio: I held overseas assignments in Latin America from 1994 – 2006. I moved from Washington D.C. to Santiago, Chile, to open offices for a global public relations firm, and led that operation for nearly five years. In 1998, I moved to Sao Paulo to manage the firm's operations in Brazil. Nearly 13 years abroad, in two very different countries and cultures, gave a wonderful perspective on life and business in this part of the world. I have three beautiful children and nag them to improve their Portuguese and Spanish (English they get at school) every chance I can.

Liesl Riddle: I am the Associate Dean for MBA Programs and Associate Professor of International Business and International Affairs at The George Washington University (GW) in Washington, D.C. My particular area of expertise is diaspora community investment and development, which I have been researching and writing about now for more than 15 years. In addition to teaching undergraduate and graduate courses on the subject, I also serve on the United Nations' advisory panel on diaspora investment and entrepreneurial policies. My educational background is in Middle Eastern Studies, which I supplemented with an MBA in Marketing/International Business and a PhD in Sociology.

Gus Tate: I graduated from Princeton in 2008 then taught English for two years at a middle school in Guangdong Province. I'm currently in my second year of a three-year master's program in Applied Linguistics/ Teaching Chinese as a Foreign Language at Beijing Normal University.

Kate Triggs: I'm British by birth, married to an American, and the mother of five-year-old twins. In my 20+ year career, I have worked in London and New York, but am now Executive Director of the Mubadala Development Company in Abu Dhabi, UAE. My current team is home to ten different nationalities and my greatest source of pride is the string of international protégés developed over my career who are now doing great things all across the globe.

Rebecca Weiner: After graduating from Yale in 1985, I began working for the US Department of State as an interpreter's assistant in Chinese, eventually becoming a senior simultaneous conference interpreter at the UN and for heads of state, film stars and CEOs. In 1995, I opted to join the business world, working for BellSouth and then Burson-Marsteller. I now co-own Strebesana Resources, a consulting firm that brokers medical optics deals between the US and China, and consult for other firms and not-for-profits. I authored the *Go Global!* chapter on China.

Hailey Weiss: I'm an undergrad at Wharton pursuing an education in marketing and communications. For the last year I have been a research assistant at Wharton's Future of Advertising Project. I pride myself on my drive, focus and ability to integrate knowledge from my classes, work and personal experience to innovatively solve problems. Outside school and work I enjoy time with family, friends and of course my dogs. Being a Colorado native I enjoy time outdoors, especially on the tennis court. I currently captain the University of Pennsylvania's Club Tennis Team.

Perry Yeatman: I started off my international career in public relations in Singapore and then moved to Moscow and London with Burson-Marsteller. From there, I went "in-house" with Unilever as a Vice President of Corporate Affairs for North America, moving over to Kraft Foods in 2005, where I now serve as Senior Vice President, Corporate Affairs, and President, The Kraft Foods Foundation. I'm lucky I get to work closely with the Chairman and CEO Irene Rosenfeld, as well as pursue my passions in community involvement and global public policy. In 2007, I co-authored *Get Ahead by Going Abroad* with Stacie.

Michael Zhu: I grew up in China and studied technology and business at Beijing University of A&A and Carnegie Mellon. I was an expat in Beijing for two years working on integrating 3Com's China joint venture and managing sales. Today as director of a global team I am based in Boston and travel often to our R&D operation in China to architect innovative technology solutions for HP's largest customers. I am a guest speaker at MBA classes at Boston's Bentley University on global alliance and collaborations, and enjoy bringing my MP100 badminton racket along on China trips to challenge the best players.

How this Book is Organized

This book is organized into seven chapters. Although it's written for the young professional, it includes plenty of information relevant to those still in high school through to seasoned professionals looking to go global. If you're just beginning to think about an international career, start at the beginning. If you're at the stage of building and communicating your global brand, go to Chapters 3 and 4. For those even remotely interested in China, don't miss Chapter 7. Everyone should check out the Go Global! video link in Chapter 1.

Each chapter includes practical tips throughout with Top Tips listed at the end of each chapter. It also includes anecdotes and stories from a variety of global thinkers, with the objective of helping you do the following:

Chapter 1: Recognizing that Global Is Everywhere

- Understand the many impacts of globalization, how it will affect your career, and the rewards available to skilled global workers.
- Appreciate that global opportunities abound both at home and abroad, and that most of us begin our international careers without leaving our home country; and if you do move abroad, it doesn't necessarily mean forever.

Chapter 2: Appreciating the Importance of a Global Mindset

- Assess whether and how an international career can work for you by understanding the skills you will need and the challenges of working cross-culturally.
- Understand that "going global" at its heart is a mindset, and learn how to think globally in everything you do so that you can recognize all kinds of international opportunities when they arise.

Chapter 3: Building Your International Qualifications

- Make the most of your undergraduate and graduate years to learn skills and gain credentials relevant to global success from your choice of classes to your selection of summer activities, for each one can make a difference.

- Learn what organizations are looking for in global workers.

- Learn about the pros and cons of volunteer vacations, internships and assignments and how your first valuable international experience might be unpaid.

- Recognize that there are risks involved in travelling, studying, volunteering, working and living abroad, and that you must understand the inherent dangers as well as be prepared for the unexpected.

Chapter 4: Creating a Winning Global Job-search Toolkit: Resumes, Cover Letters and Elevator Pitches

- Package your experience appropriately for each market, industry and company you apply to.

- Learn how to incorporate international experience and interests into your job-search toolkit, e.g., resumes, cover letters and interview preparation.

- Understand the importance of personal branding and the valuable role social media plays.

Chapter 5: Pulling It All Together: Ready, Set...Go Global!

- Develop a career-search strategy based on guided research, including gathering intelligence, networking and targeted study and analysis of relevant markets, industries and companies.

- Look beyond corporate positions alone to review options in the not-for-profit and government sectors.

- Understand the range of options in international jobs so that you can manage your expectations and be prepared.

Chapter 6: Launching an International Career

- Evaluate the possibilities of moving to another country without first securing a job.

- Appreciate the legal and practical complexities of working overseas: visas, banking, insurance, taxes and other official requirements.

- Turn your first international job into an international career.

Chapter 7: Navigating the Pathways to China

- Understand China's current job market, including why its market is bifurcated and challenging.

- Differentiate yourself among the competition looking toward Asia as the new "land of opportunity."

- Appreciate the variety of pathways to China, including working for MNCs and Chinese organizations; going the corporate, not-for-profit or education route; transferring in or moving on your own; and starting a business in China.

- Know where to turn for additional information and resources to prepare you before you go and help you while you're on the ground living in China.

Go Global!

Chapter 1

Recognizing that
Global is Everywhere

> If you're wondering why globalization is important, check out this video filled with startling facts and figures about why going global is so important today: http://youtu.be/Y4tKZ1hUOoU

Globalization is everywhere today. You can hardly turn on the news or read an op-ed without hearing how our world is growing smaller and more interconnected. Some worry about this trend, others welcome it, and many seem to do both at once.

On the scary side, we read about global warming, global population growth and epidemic outbreaks that now must be evaluated globally due to global travel. We face the fact that the global financial crisis we're still suffering from was sparked in part by how interconnected the global economy is. We watch China, India, Brazil and other countries recover much faster than the US – and we witness Americans streaming abroad to look for work, a reversal of trends that brought many of our parents or grandparents to America.

Yet the positives of globalization are also legion. We watch global sports and cultural events. We buy inexpensive imported goods, and maybe cash paychecks from companies doing exports. We enjoy cultural globalization by watching Japanimation or Bollywood, dancing to Afro pop, LatAm or Reggaeton, or sampling the latest global "fusion" food trend. And we know the same interconnectedness that can cause global crises can also bring about local miracles, like tiny fair-trade craft circles selling products around the world via blog, democracy protesters sharing information on Twitter and banks raising micro-business start-up funds via internet penny-investors.

Young people, whether they're just getting out of college or have been out there for a year or two, I say to them, take a chance, take a risk. You don't know what opportunities lie outside your home town, unless you give it a chance. So whether you want to focus on a developing country in Latin America or in Asia or a more developed country, say the United Kingdom, give it a chance, give it a go. Now is the time to explore new opportunities that might be much more difficult to explore 10 years, 15 years out. – **Curtis S. Chin**

Global Perspective and Its Impact on Careers

Whatever they think of globalization, nearly everyone agrees it is here now and happening, faster every year, so all of us – especially students – will need to figure out how to deal with it. Employers understand that globalization is here to stay. They want and need globally-minded employees and executives. In our ever-shrinking world, global experience will continue to move from "nice" to "must-have" as a driver for career success. Witness:

- The National Association for Study Abroad (NASA) released its results of a November 2010 public opinion survey of a broad cross-section of Americans on the importance of international education:
  - 57% said international education is essential to the educational experience.
  - 65% agreed that if young people do not learn foreign languages, they will be at a competitive career disadvantage.
  - 73% believe that higher education institutions must do a better job of teaching students about the world if they are to be prepared to compete in the global economy.
- Online job sites like GlobalCareers, SimplyHired and The Ladders have added specific sections seeking managers with global skills.
- Sites like GoingGlobal specialize 100% in global careers.
- Study-abroad programs shift to less traditional destinations, such as China, India and Brazil.

As globalization continues to shift the playing field away from a US- or Western-led business model to a truly global one, young professionals must adapt. Organizations need people who can operate globally, so students must build their international skill set for success. – **Stacie Berdan**

Which of the following curricular approaches does your MBA program employ to cultivate a deeper global mindset in your students? (check all that apply)

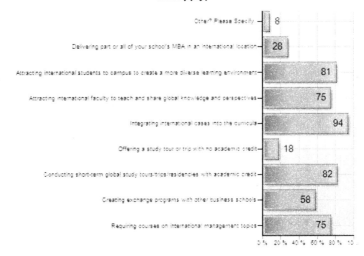

Source: MBA Roundtable 2009

- The US education system is still a major magnet for global talent, but many educators fear a slowdown in foreign students applying to US MBA and other programs in favor of more globally-focused universities in Europe and Asia, especially China.

- MBA programs are rapidly increasing international courses, language proficiency, and semester abroad requirements in hopes of producing more employable graduates.

  Our members know they need it, and their Executive MBA programs seem to be the most innovative as they leverage international partnerships, infuse curriculum with international cases and faculty, and have greater access to visiting business leaders. Full-time MBA programs are starting to adopt this model and it's a great start.
  – ***Carleen Kertulla***

The ability to work globally and cross-culturally may make the difference between a satisfying career of progressive success, and an ongoing struggle.

Faster recovery outside the US further complicates the picture for young Americans. The fastest growth is not coming from yesterday's "plum" markets like the UK, Germany or Switzerland. China surpassed Japan as the world's second largest economy even before the triple threat of earthquake-tsunami-nuclear radiation affected Japan's GDP growth. Some economists predict that China will overtake the US to become the world's top economy by 2020, while others argue that demographic and other issues will hold China back.

All agree, however, that the sleeping giant has finally awakened. Emerging markets, such as Brazil, India and Russia, also offer far more rapid growth than mature markets like the US, EU or Japan.

The stakes for new graduates are high. Jobless rates hover around nine percent across the US, with estimates as high as 40% for new graduates looking for professional work. Our schools must do a better job at preparing our students for the global marketplace. **– Stacie Berdan**

Are we adequately preparing students for a global marketplace?

Globalization Crosses Professions

Globalization affects not just business students, but most students looking to enter the workforce. Budding scientists may end up in a new research lab in India. Communications majors might do social media strategy for consumer products in China. Educators may receive grants to research foreign language development in European children. Liberal arts majors may work on campaigns supporting healthy eating in Brazil. The possibilities are endless. Now more than ever, global mindedness is critical to professional success.

The same is true for employers. I urge you not to limit yourself by thinking "business is not for me," or "I'm not the government type." By doing so you may miss your career-launching dream job. You will be well served to pay attention to all sorts of global job opportunities.

*When I look at the senior leadership of Dupont today, 60% of us have lived overseas. I spent 5 years in Europe in the early 90s, running a business and running a manufacturing operation. That number is going to 100% in the not-too-distant future. – **Diane Gulyas***

The global economy is here. Those who know how to play in it have a better chance of succeeding. Today's organizations seek people who can succeed in the global marketplace and have gained international experience, interests and/or foreign language skills. Such skills can be a huge differentiator if you have them.

Studies show that younger Americans are already embracing the need for global awareness. A December 2009 Kelly Workforce survey found that of adults between the ages of 18-28:

- 81% believe it is important to their career prospects that they become more globally oriented.
- 67% have recently worked closely with colleagues from a different country or culture.
- 82% feel that they possess the skills to work in a more globally-oriented workplace.
- In deciding where to work, exposure to a global environment is considered "extremely important" by 32%.
- Only 35% get formal cross-cultural/language training from employers.

Clearly, global skills will put you ahead of the pack.

*In a rapidly globalized world, our generation either becomes international players – or we're left behind. – **Robbie Fried, CLI***

What impact has globalization had on today's workforce?

Changing Patterns in International Career Opportunities

As globalization expands, the organizations involved with it – corporations, non-profit organizations and government agencies – are changing how they view and who they send for international positions.

- Global, virtual teams are becoming the norm. Many international jobs begin – perhaps even remain – in the home country or headquarters of an organization.
- Less senior managers are being sent. Due to the high costs of relocating senior employees, and the need to groom more global employees, companies now prefer transferring junior people.
- These junior professionals typically receive minimal packages, sometimes only a work visa, a round-trip plane ticket, and a contact on the ground who will hire them locally.
- Language proficiency matters. Both language skills and experience in a culture or country have played an increasingly important role in international transfers.
- Short-term assignments are becoming the norm. Organizations now need people on the ground for three-, six- or nine-month assignments rather than the traditional multi-year ones; junior staff who have proven themselves are often sent instead.

These changes reflect the big issues of cost, competence and value; even senior people working overseas may receive lower benefit packages than their predecessors. Organizations know they need more global workers, but aren't going to spend too much extra to get them. This is where new arrivals come in. Recent graduates with portfolios that reflect international exposure and experience will be ideally positioned to benefit from these new opportunities in the global marketplace. International exposure can help you:

- Land a job on graduation.
- Shift from a local to a global job.
- Fast-track you to a senior position.
- Increase compensation.
- Provide challenging, interesting assignments in growth sectors.
- Get the attention and respect of senior management and peers.
- Offer a great lifestyle with lots of fun along the way.

Many people told me not to go overseas. They said that I'd go abroad and HQs would forget about me. I didn't initially go because I wanted to get ahead at DuPont, I went because I was fascinated by different cultures. It ended up catapulting my career. – **Diane Gulyas**

Shifting Trends in the Global Marketplace

Many organizations I work with are sending employees abroad for international training and exposure during the US economic downturn. Packages aren't as generous as they once were, and Euro-driven countries no longer top the list, but the results are the same: Increased global experience for employees and the company, preparing both for a global economy less dominated than it once was by the US

Published statistics don't always reflect this trend, largely because companies are changing how they send employees. To cut costs – and emphasize the global nature of these assignments – companies today offer fewer "expat packages," those where the employee stays on HQ's payroll with HQ benefits. Instead, "global workers" are increasingly being hired as local employees in countries where the employer sees growth. But long-term benefits for the worker are the same: Resume and skill-building experience gained by working globally.

Another exciting new twist is the rise of foreign-owned companies enticing American workers to live and work in growth markets like China, Brazil, Mexico, Southern Africa and Eastern Europe. These mid- to large-scale companies appreciate the value of native English skills and a Western education, and so are importing or hiring locally from among the growing number of young professionals who have moved to these high-growth markets. For the company, these hires mean affordable international intellectual capital. For the workers, these jobs mean international exposure and the introductory experience that can help launch a global career.

In fact some countries like Russia, Brazil, Malaysia and the U.A.E. are using the US economic crisis to actively entice their own expatriate talent home, reversing a "brain drain" that for many started generations ago. Many countries are reminding compatriots that their economy is booming while the US lags. China, in particular, has been trying to attract its citizens back for decades, and recently accelerated efforts via a "Medium- and Long-Term Talent Development Plan" (2010-2020) designed to bring China-born scientists age 35 and under home. India is also coaxing home foreign-trained scientists via grant programs and support for social networking exchanges. In fact, there's growing evidence that the complicated and restrictive US visa and immigration policies are accelerating this "reverse brain drain."

Where do you think the greatest career opportunities are by country?

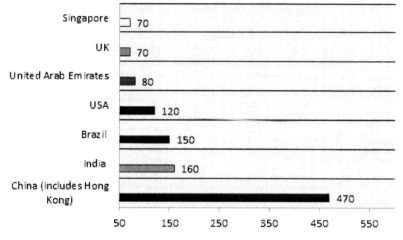

Source: Go Global! Survey 2011

Globally savvy Americans are benefiting from "reverse brain drain" right along with the Indians, Chinese, Russians and others. Brazil, for instance, envisions tremendous growth and invests twice the percentage of its annual GDP in science and technology as its average Latin American neighbor. Government-led investment in green energy has made that a major growth area for Brazil. Both government and business recognize that Brazil's education system must change to close the rich-poor income gap that limits economic growth. Despite some mixed reviews of the government's reform movement's successes,

Brazilian innovation is expected to skyrocket within the next 10 years – and with it, opportunities for Americans as well as Brazilians.

> *Several important trends are making Brazilian employers increasingly access global talent. For multinationals, Brazil is a market where they must be successful; it is a priority geography for nearly every FORTUNE 100 company and many others. These companies invest vital resources – including human capital – to assure their competitiveness. The market is also a perfect training ground for future corporate leadership that will need to understand emerging markets. We see many industries, such as automotive, technology, financial services and energy, cycle "fast track" talent through the Brazilian market to build their management skills in preparation for larger, global roles.* – **Ramiro Prudencio**

Similar examples abound elsewhere, but news on these opportunities is not yet commonplace in the US media; you have to look for it. Some of the largest MNCs are based in China, Brazil, India, Mexico and U.A.E. Already, some of the greatest increases in hiring in 2011 can be found in China, Hong Kong/China, India, Russia and Dubai. In the meantime, unemployment rates increased in the United States, UK, Netherlands, Spain and Italy. Tracking these global job/hiring rates annually is critical. Times have changed, and will keep changing – and so must your approach to finding a global job.

- The Forbes Global 2000 list of 2008 included no Chinese companies in the top 25; in 2009 China had four of the top 25.
- In 2005, American firms held 14 of the top 25 slots in the Forbes Global 2000; five years later they were down to 10.
- In the 2010 Fortune 500 global list, China had three in the top 10; the US only had two.

"Go West, young man" was popular advice for young adults 150 years ago as America's West offered land, minerals and burgeoning trade. "Go Global!" is today's best advice for the current generation of talented and ambitious opportunity seekers. Proper planning and preparation will make a difference and so we wrap up this first chapter with some key principles on preparing to Go Global. All of these will be explored further in the following chapters.

Top Tips for Dealing with a Global World

- Learn to think globally and cross-culturally.
- Acquire international/multicultural experience.
- Master at least one foreign language, starting as early as you can.
- Cultivate listening skills and other personal traits that enhance cross-cultural interaction.
- Do your research, and never stop learning.
- Network. Network. Network.
- Find good mentors, learning when to listen and when to break away.
- Monitor global business trends, especially in your chosen field.
- Minimize school debt to allow for greater flexibility upon graduation.
- Don't be afraid to take calculated risks.
- Know that global jobs sometimes begin on home turf.
- Be prepared for the ups and downs of going global.
- Emphasize your international skills to the same degree that you do your experience.

Chapter 2

Appreciating the Importance of a Global Mindset

> The ability to work successfully across cultures is critical to a successful international career. To hear Perry Yeatman, a senior business leader, describe the importance of a global mindset for today's workforce, visit: http://youtu.be/Tvw2IPkglUg

Once you know the value of Going Global, as discussed in Chapter 1, the next step is to assess your own readiness – how prepared you are to operate in an international environment. Some of you may have doubts about moving abroad and would prefer to start out in the US It helps, though, to understand what distinguishes a global thinker.

Ask academics, business professionals or government bureaucrats to describe "global mindset" and most will offer similar definitions: An ability to work successfully across cultures (not necessarily in another country). Experts disagree, however, about what makes one person better prepared than another to do this and whether a global mindset can actually be taught.

What Is a Global Mindset?

Having a global mindset requires not only possessing the technical skills necessary for operating successfully in an international environment, but also the personal skills necessary for applying these effectively. From Wikipedia: "In its broadest sense, an expatriate is any person living in a country other than the one where he or she is a citizen. In common usage, the term often describes professionals sent abroad by their companies, as opposed to locally-hired staff, who can also be foreigners. The differentiation found in common usage usually comes down to socio-economic factors, so skilled professionals working in another country are described as expatriates, whereas a manual laborer who has moved to another country to earn more money tends to be labeled an 'immigrant'."

Much new research on "global mindset" is being led by Thunderbird School of Global Management. Its rigorous, scientific study of the drivers of expat success has shown that a global mindset crosses professions and countries. In its report, Conceptualizing and Measuring Global Mindset®: Development of the Global Mindset Inventory[1], The Thunderbird Global Mindset Institute's team provides extensive detail on the topic. I had the pleasure of meeting and interviewing Dr. Mansour Javidan for an article that I wrote for *Today's Campus* on Global Mindset; the article includes the following breakdown of the global mindset:

- **Intellectual capital:** Defined as knowledge of global industry and competitors and is measured by knowledge of global business savvy, cognitive complexity, cosmopolitan outlook.
- **Social capital:** Involves building trusting relationships and is measured by intercultural empathy, interpersonal impact, and diplomacy.
- **Psychological capital** reflects and is measured by one's passion for diversity, quest for adventure, and self-assurance.

At the most basic level, global mindset is about skills that are proven to work cross-culturally. In 2006, I conducted a survey with more than 200 professionals who had successfully worked overseas to

---

[1]http://www.thunderbird.edu/wwwfiles/pdf/knowledge_network/ctrs_excellence/global_mindset_leadership_institute/gmi-tech-report.pdf

inform my first book, *Get Ahead By Going Abroad*. Respondents identified five traits deemed critical in cross-cultural situations:

- **Adaptability/Flexibility**: Style-flexing is key. Internationalists must appreciate cultural differences and tolerate ambiguity. In foreign environments you must be fluid, able to work around and find "other ways" to accomplish tasks. Problem-solving abilities are crucial. In global jobs, you must be able to solve complex problems in many different ways, adapting the way you analyze and resolve issues to the situation you are working in.

- **Excellent Communication:** How you speak, listen, and intuit can make or break a global experience. Your ability to understand and make yourself understood is critical when differences in language, culture, politics and religion increase odds of miscommunications. Non-verbal cues, such as culture, body language, reading between the lines, and interpreting the environment, are all important.

- **Building teams and relationships:** Internationalists look beyond stereotypes and get to know people as individuals, and appreciate the rewards of bringing together different individuals. This requires the solid organizational, time and people-management skills that are key at home, but also the ability to reach across cultures and draw people from different backgrounds together. Good global teamwork enhances your success – and your team's.

- **Patience and persistence:** Successful global workers maintain grace under pressure, going with the flow when nothing works as they expect. "Local time" and "local custom" mean different things in every market. Savvy internationalists know that waiting and watching often outperforms rushing in demanding immediate answers or changes. Long-term results count most.

- **Intellectual curiosity:** Good global workers are interested in and open to dealing with whatever comes their way, and enjoy new environments. This curiosity drives internationalists to learn about the world – history, geography, literature, economics. Knowledge, in turn, leads to a better understanding of how to work across cultures. Global workers are curious about what makes business tick, and that leads to strong and growing business acumen.

Although these traits may be inherent in some, you can learn them. If you're serious about going global, start practicing these skills in personal and professional situations today. You'll find that while these skills are critical to success abroad, they will also help you succeed here at home. In the global marketplace, technical skills are necessary but not sufficient. Global workers also need cultural sensitivity, the ability to interpret situations, information and facts while being empathetic and diplomatic team players, and a passionate curiosity that lets them enjoy the cultural diversity they thrive in every day.

The global worker fulfills an organization's needs. Companies, not-for-profits and government agencies expect cross-cultural abilities in their new hires as much as they expect basic professional skills.

Is Going Global Right for You?

So if this is what makes successful international workers, how do you know if you can be one of them? Living and working globally is not for everyone.

95% of the 200 professionals I surveyed prior to writing "Get Ahead By Going Abroad" agreed that not everyone can successfully live and work abroad. Be honest with yourself, take a few self-evaluations, and talk to people who know you and understand global careers. – **Stacie Berdan**

Only you can tell whether or not you have the curiosity, openness and interest in the world to succeed in a global career. You may enjoy international experiences, but never have been tested in a global work environment. You may have travelled, but not had to cope with deadlines or real work pressure overseas. Maybe your study abroad experience was terrific – but also cocooned you against the toughest challenges of your host culture. No matter where you rate your own global mindset or how many of the five traits of successful globetrotters you have, before considering an international job search, ask yourself: Is a global assignment right for me?

To help you begin to answer that question, here is a thought exercise based on my research on successful internationalists.

Begin by thinking about a time in your life – preferably recently – when you felt stretched or challenged. It could be an athletic competition, the first day on the job or campus, the presentation of your thesis or your first client meeting. Remember the stresses and disappointments of that experience as well as its triumphs and rewards. Now imagine that event further complicated by language, cultural differences, exotic food or anything else that makes you nervous about international exchange. Take time to fully imagine yourself in that situation. How well would you have been able to deal with it? Be honest here; you're fooling no one but yourself if you aren't.

Now it's time to rate yourself as honestly as you can, on a scale of 1 (low) to 10 (high) on how much you agree with each of the following:

- I thrive on challenges – the more the better.
- I enjoy meeting and getting to know new people.
- I love new places, new foods, and new cultures.
- I can get along with many different personalities, including people others find difficult.
- I thrive on change, and am happy to be surrounded by it 24/7.
- I enjoy taking calculated risks.
- I don't get bothered by things that seem different or strange.
- I don't mind being alone.
- I go the extra mile – time and again – without being asked.
- I thrive when asked to go outside my comfort zone.
- I am curious about what makes the world go round.
- I am adaptable.
- I am a good listener and communicator.
- I like working in teams.
- I can handle failure and learn from it.

Add up your score. Give yourself five points for having bought this book! That by itself shows a curiosity that can be built on. If your total "score" was 120 or above, you may have a bright global future ahead of you – just remember, the best cross-cultural workers never stop honing their global thinking skills. If you scored 90-119, you have the makings of a good internationalist, and a guide to areas where you need to brush up. If you scored 51-89, think seriously before you apply for international jobs, and consider how much you can evolve. If you scored 50 or below, you probably aren't well suited for an international career **at this time.** If so, it's better to know that BEFORE you invest too much time and effort in trying to build one. But keep in mind that people's scores on assessments tend to change over time, especially as your pathway through life becomes molded by real-life experience.

Understanding – and Preparing for – Culture Shock

One of the most widely discussed and often misunderstood aspects of international work is culture shock. Culture shock is the confusion, disorientation and emotional upheaval that comes from immersion in a new culture. Culture shock often follows a three-phased cycle starting with a honeymoon period where everything feels grand. Fabulous turns to frustration, depression and confusion, often triggered by an event involving minor cultural differences. All usually ends well as the recovery phase smoothes the crinkles enabling a wiser you to move on. International newbies are often either overly optimistic ("*I* won't have any trouble adjusting") or overly pessimistic ("everyone takes 6 months to get used to the basics before they can do anything productive").

In fact, almost everyone who works internationally experiences some degree of culture shock with every major cultural transition – whether moving to a new culture, or dealing with a new cultural group or sub-culture at home. You can experience a type of culture shock if you are immersed in virtual team work, working global hours on global projects. Whatever your encounters are, everyone who works internationally needs to develop coping mechanisms.

Experienced internationalists learn to recognize their own patterns of adjustment to new experiences. They come to appreciate the coping mechanisms that work best for them. By giving themselves the space, time and other support they need to adjust, they smooth their own transitions and develop their own culture shock absorbers, so they can continue working productively.

I find that some of the most effective principles to deal with culture shock include:
- *Assume differences until similarity is proven.*
- *Relate to individuals, not a "culture."*
- *Work with a culture rather than against it.*
- *Ask "What do I need to understand?" not what should I do*
- *Listen and observe, think and then talk.*
- *Focus on the benefits of differences rather than simply trying to avoid mistakes.*
- *Never try to "go native."*   **– Terry Brake**

Savvy global workers also remember that the toughest bouts of culture shock often happen when transitioning "home." This reverse culture shock or re-entry shock also requires coping – and preparation.

I'll never forget the first time I came back to the US after 3 years in China. Everything seemed so huge! The cars, the houses, the food packages, the people – it felt overwhelming, and seemed so insanely wasteful I had to work not to judge my fellow Americans as hopelessly corrupt. – **Rebecca Weiner**

If you find culture shock a constant, awful strain that gets worse rather than better with each transition, take it as a warning sign. Like subsequent ripples from a stone being thrown in a pond, the height and frequency of culture shock waves should diminish with time.

Being a Woman

My first book focused on the benefits of women working abroad, and so it's only natural that I should include some tips to get a better handle on what it's like being a woman working abroad. If you're interested in reading the whole story, you should pick up a copy of **Get Ahead By Going Abroad**. The vast majority of women I interviewed for that book (and hundreds more since) agree that, as a woman:

- If you're good at what you do, you will be accepted in international business circles as a professional first.

- There are many professional advantages to being a female. Most describe themselves as highly visible and so they leveraged it.

- Some countries, of course, do not treat women as equals. Each must be assessed individually. For example, in some Muslim countries, women do not have the same legal rights as men, nor the same business responsibilities. They have different customs for dating. Do not judge, condemn or compare your own culture in a more favorable light in public. Take care of how you dress so as not to offend or draw unnecessary attention to you.

- There are benefits to being married or single, having children or not. Women have done it before, and *Get Ahead By Going Abroad* can be an excellent resource for you.

- Safety must be considered first. Women overseas must be cautious, attentive and not take chances when it comes to personal safety. Other cultures will have impressions of "what American women are like." Whether they're accurate or not, you need to know those perceptions and anticipate them.

Abiding by Safe Travel Tips is critical:
- Find out which countries/cities are considered dangerous for women.

- Understand that in some countries, women do not have the same rights as men.

- Know and follow the local laws.

- Be conscious of what you wear, both clothes and jewelry.

- Don't walk alone at night; stay in groups.

- Keep cash stashed on your person.

- Don't be caught by surprise; be aware of your surroundings.
- Err on the side of caution with strangers.
- Don't arrive late at night to a place you don't know or fear might be dangerous.
- Keep your cell phone charged at all times.
- Sexual misinterpretation happens to most women who spend time in other cultures. There are many reasons; be prepared for it to happen – and to respond properly.

We have preconceived notions of people of other cultures. Be patient and work carefully to show your culture, and learn about others.

Safety Issues Abroad

There are inherent risks involved in traveling, studying, working and living abroad, and you have to be prepared to face them. Natural disasters can hit anywhere – and can be aggravated by inferior infrastructures typically found in poorer countries. Some disasters, such as earthquakes, hurricanes and volcanic eruptions, may be more common abroad than at home. Political unrest and uprisings can happen as we have seen in Egypt, Tunisia, Libya and Syria. Americans overseas can be cut off from easy contact with friends and families back home, despite the best laid plans. Are you ready for that? Much can go wrong overseas, from unwanted sexual advances to financial disasters (including budget-busting stupidity).

If you find yourself obsessed with fear of such issues, working overseas is probably not right for you. But even if you feel comfortable with risk, you still must think about safety. Whether you are moving abroad or taking a quick business trip – even personal travel – make sure you understand the inherent dangers. Plan ahead, and know where to turn for help if you need it:

- The US Department of State issues travel advisory site cautions and up-to-date information underscoring the importance of remaining vigilant and security conscious in specific countries.

- The US Department of State offers safe travel tips, a comprehensive list of action steps to take both before you depart and while traveling.
- The Centers for Disease Control and Prevention (CDC) web site provides detailed information on healthy traveling, from disease outbreaks and required immunizations to food and water safety. Always get a physical before heading overseas – even if only for a few months – and bring a full supply of prescriptions with doctor's note of explanation. Confirm health insurance coverage outside the US, including that your insurance covers medical evacuation services (Medevac).
- Travel and living abroad books and websites offer valuable health and safety information about specific locations.

Also, pay attention to common-sense safety:
- **Be Aware of Potential Anti-American sentiments:** Keep a low-profile. Register with the US Embassy or Consulate, use the buddy system, and keep your family/friends appraised of your whereabouts, especially while traveling.
- **Valuables:** Bring little and carry a copy of your passport photo page – not your passport unless the situation requires it. Email yourself a copy of your passport and any other important information, such as credit card numbers and bank accounts so that if any are lost or stolen, you can go online and get a copy. Use a money belt and stick small bills in pockets for quick purchases.
- **Financials:** Manage your money, know what things cost, do not wave your money around and stick to your budget (running out of cash is risky business).
- **Smart determination:** Living in foreign environments challenges and tires even the most determined. Be prepared to stick with it, but know when to call it quits if negatives outweigh positives.

Be aware that our definitions of right and wrong or "how things work" are culturally determined. Your ideas about acceptable laws, gender roles and other aspects of daily life may differ from local rules. You don't have to participate in or approve behaviors you disagree with, but be prepared that your only choice may be to walk away.

Thinking Globally – Strengthening YOUR Global Mindset

To recap, you must think globally, whether you want to work in Warsaw or if you aspire to manage a global, virtual team from Miami. You must pay attention to international business trends, world events and global politics, and you have to strengthen your international business acumen. Practice working in cross-cultural situations and strengthen your social skills. I wrap up this chapter with a short list of practical tips to enhance your global thinking and skills. Via these channels, you will build your "global resume" as well as your global skill set, and be ready to seek a career-launching international job.

Top Tips for Enhancing Your Global Persona

- Hone your cross-cultural skills.
- Pay attention to world events.
- Monitor business trends.
- Practice foreign languages.
- Monitor apps and blogs.
- Join local and virtual international clubs.
- Pay attention to hot regions and issues you care about.
- Find a support group.
- Travel abroad.
- Study abroad.
- Seek a short-term job abroad.

Chapter 3

Building Your International Qualifications

In the following two photo essays, you can hear from two young professionals, Kelly Loughlin, about the importance of her study abroad experience and her tips for you: http://youtu.be/H1r5q6fdiPc, and from Rosary Abot, who was inspired to research ethical behavior among students across countries during her time studying abroad: http://youtu.be/SVGZ-vE1VDA

You know the value of going global, and you've honestly assessed your ability to succeed in a global career. The next step is building your global credentials. We'll talk later about writing a resume and other job-seeking materials that appeal to organizations looking for internationally-minded candidates. But before you develop your resume, you must first build your international qualifications.

The earlier you start the better. Your global mindset can begin at home, before you apply for a passport or step out of the country. Foreign language studies begun in college are good, those in high school better, those begun in elementary school better yet, and bilingualism from birth best of all. Obviously, you didn't choose your parents or what they exposed you to as a kid. But from high school on, you can make choices that will help you stand out from the pack. Language study and other global coursework, globally-oriented extra-curricular activities, time abroad, internships, even having international friends will all make huge differences when you job-hunt. Smart choices about where you go to school and how you fund your education can give you flexibility in global experiences not open to those burdened with debt.

I will cover a broad range of topics, each of which can be approached differently, depending on whether you're in high school, studying as an undergrad or grad student, or already a graduate.

Master English Communications

In a world of 140-character tweets and OMG! texting abbreviations, communicating well in English, both written and spoken, seems to be a dying art. But it is an important skill for every career, and so you must focus on your ability to speak, write and present succinctly. You need to be able to back up your arguments with rational and relevant points. If you need practice speaking, join Toastmasters or practice making presentations with your friends and professors. To that end, don't shy away from, but actively seek out, courses that will hone your expository writing skills, courses in world literature, history, or political science, for example, that will both develop your analytic skills and teach you a little more about the world outside the US

Foreign Language Learning

The benefits of learning a foreign language are vast. Of course, knowing a second language allows you to communicate with speakers of that language. It helps you better understand other cultures, since language and culture are invariably intertwined. Studies show that learning a foreign language strengthens other academic areas as well – including proficiency in your mother tongue.[2] Neuroscience is exploring how language learning shapes memories, perceptions, and basic patterns of thought. The quote long attributed to Charlemagne sums it up best: "To have a second language is to have a second soul."

Students today, particularly students growing up in the United States, sometimes really don't have the language skills that will help them build a career both inside the United States but certainly outside the United States. So even as they're studying economics, trade policy and marketing,

---

[2] http://actfl.org/i4a/pages/index.cfm?pageid=4524

I'd say take the time to also study Spanish, study a foreign language, because you'll never go wrong in a meeting with someone who speaks a language other than English to have a little bit of a conversation. Even if you're not fluent in Spanish or Japanese or Chinese, the effort that you made in college or right out of college to understand someone's culture, someone's language, can only help you go further in building relationships that are so important to building a global career. – **Curtis S. Chin**

US Lags in Foreign Language Education

Despite these clear advantages, the United States has fallen behind in foreign language training in relation to its own past and to other countries, according to many studies. The US is the only industrialized nation where many – if not most – high schools and colleges still grant degrees with zero foreign language requirements. Even those with requirements often accept just a year or two of foreign language study, a minimal proficiency level that won't get graduates far in the global marketplace.

There's an old joke – sad but too true: You call someone who speaks three languages trilingual and someone who speaks two languages bilingual, so what do you call someone who speaks just one language? American. – **Rebecca Weiner**

We are very concerned that at a time when business leaders are calling for employees who can communicate and understand the cultures of our business partners around the world, the statistics point out that our students are woefully underprepared to meet these demands.
– **Marty Abbott**

If anything, smaller percentages of Americans are studying foreign languages now than in the past. The American Council on Teaching Foreign Language (ACTFL) reported that 32% of students in public secondary schools were enrolled in language classes in 2007-08, and 18.5 % overall in K-12.

According to a 2006 Modern Language Association report, only 8.6% of US students were studying foreign languages, down from

16.5% in 1965. These numbers are likely to worsen now that Congress has cut funding for the Foreign Language Assistance Program.

Meantime, the competitive global marketplace is increasingly well-stocked with multilingual talent. Europeans often graduate college tri-lingual. Most Chinese graduate speaking, arguably, the world's two most important business languages, Mandarin and English. Latin Americans often speak Spanish, English and, increasingly, Portugese. This is your future competition. Are you prepared?

> *50% of the professionals I surveyed while writing this book said that "Do you speak a foreign language?" is one of the top four questions they ask of potential hires.* – **Stacie Berdan**

> *One experience I wasn't expecting in college was having my first day of Spanish class with grad students. I was still getting lost on campus! It was sort of terrifying, at age 17, to walk into a classroom with students three to five years older than me. I thought for sure my placement in a class on Spanish translation must've been a mistake. But the administration insisted that I had tested out of all the classes on learning the language and eventually I realized I deserved to be there. In the end I did just as well as the people going for their masters. More importantly, I was proud of myself and thankful for everything that I'd learned in my elementary and high school education.* – **Beth Cubanski**

Standing Out

The good news is that Americans who take the trouble to master a foreign language can really stand out.

> *As I applied for internships, in every single interview I was questioned about my languages. I've been asked which ones I speak, how long I studied, have I ever been out of the country. Employers love to see that you are culturally aware. Foreign languages are becoming essential to succeed in in the future. Bon chance!* – **Ben Paulker**

This differentiation matters today, and will matter even more in the future. As businesses expand their international operations, hiring managers want employees with solid language and cross-cultural skills.

Government and not-for-profit organizations also prefer candidates with the language and cultural skills to work across boundaries. The

US government is so desperate for Americans with these skills that it is helping to grow them, via programs like the National Security Education Program (NSEP), STARTALK and The Language Flagship, which recognize the importance of foreign language mastery for both competitiveness and national security. Even though FLAP has been cut, other programs continue. Many offer job opportunities to students, so these are networking as well as educational channels.

> *I want to be a doctor and I'm pretty sure I'm only the Spanish major on the pre-med track. I went into the college application process knowing I wanted to go to medical school even while I was choosing schools based on their language programs because languages apply to any career. For example, I don't think there is any hospital in the US where every patient speaks English. An emergency room doctor who speaks multiple languages would be an asset to a hospital.* – **Beth Cubanski**

Language Choice

What foreign language should you study? Any one you can! For many students, the choice is limited by what is currently being taught in their schools. But the bottom line is, any second language is better than none. Any foreign language will help "switch on" that "second soul," help you stand out, and open up expanded job opportunities.

That said, not all languages are created equal. When selecting which language to study, you should consider your personal interests, ease of learning, and future employment potential.

- **Personal interest**: If you don't like a language – or the culture it sprang from – you won't put in the hours needed to master it. No language study is fun at the beginning – there's no getting around the hours of drill. But if you like the food, poetry, movies or some other aspect of the culture, that will help pull you through.

- **Ease of learning**: All else being equal, it can help to choose a language that comes relatively easily to you. Some languages are grammar-heavy, and work best for learners who grasp rules quickly. Others require memorization of word-order rules. Still others are musical, and require intonation. Spend time flipping through first-year textbooks in different languages at a bookstore, and see which make sense to you, and which feel like smacking your head on a wall. Also, consider opportunities you to practice – are there native speakers in your area? Learner's groups?

- **Future potential**: In the end, you learn new languages to expand your opportunities. Any language will do that, but some more than others. Many Americans choose Spanish because so many classes are offered and native speakers available to practice with and jobs for bilinguals are legion. Spanish is great, but also consider looking outside that box. The languages considered "critical" by the US government (Chinese, Japanese, Russian, Arabic, Hindi, Urdu, Farsi and Portuguese) all represent massive and growing opportunities in business, cultural and governmental exchange.

Learning Mode Choice

What's the best way to learn a foreign language? Formal classroom learning is preferable if it's available. But there are also alternatives instead of and/or supplements to formal classes:

- **Language clubs**. Informal groups meet on campuses, in cultural centers, via faith-based and communities and on the internet.

- **Language-learning self-study books and software**. Many people have acquired remarkable proficiency using the likes of Rosetta Stone, Berlitz and Praxis Language.

- **Private tutoring**. One-on-one tutoring can be expensive, but also very effective. And sometimes, it can come free – in exchange for one-on-one tutoring in English. Check out bulletin boards, real and virtual, to find potential language study-buddies (just be careful about safety, as in all situations when meeting strangers!).

- **Immersion programs**. Immersion study – where everything is done in the target language – can help you leap from novice to intermediate or intermediate to fluency. They are available term-time and summertime, one-on-one and for groups, in the US and around the world, sometimes with cultural activities and home-stays. Some have been around for decades, others are new, so be sure to check out references. Programs and policies on academic credit vary, so be sure to coordinate beforehand with your school.

My daughters have studied Spanish since kindergarten. We're considering attending an immersion program in Central America in the summer between sixth and seventh grades to solidify the learning thus far – and getting to know the customs and cultures of one country in particular. – **Stacie Berdan**

Any language learning is better than no language learning. The most important thing is to start it, do it and keep it up.

I love learning languages! I feel that they have gotten me to places that I would never have been without them. They will definitely be a part of my future as well. – **Beth Cubanski**

Tips for Learning Languages

- **Invest the time.** The more time you spend immersed in the language, the faster you will learn. Be patient with yourself: many studies show learners need 50+ exposures to a new word in every form (reading, writing, speaking, listening) before it really sticks. Give yourself time to connect to the language.
- **Focus on "communicative competence."** Don't just memorize words and phrases. Language communicates, so communicate! Go to ethnic restaurants and order in your target language, visit hospitals and volunteer to help nurses communicate. Be overwhelmed, then figure it out! Use dictionaries. Build vocabulary. Play with the language.
- **Show initiative**. No one can make you learn another language. You have to want to do it to succeed. Follow your curiosity and learn the words and phrases that interest you, stimulate you. Set your own goals and work to achieve them.
- **Enjoy it!**

There are so many great websites offering tips in learning a foreign language, like those from the ACTFL.

So What Can You Do?

If You're in High School, see below. If You're an Undergrad or Grad Student skip to the next section.

Learning foreign languages comes easier the earlier you start. But don't despair if you haven't studied a foreign language by high school! You still can. Many fine high school programs provide the instructional support necessary to move toward or even attain fluency.

Choose elective language classes, remembering that most other countries REQUIRE them. If you can't, seek out after-school classes or lessons. And what about home – do any family members speak a language from the "old country"? Would your family consider hosting an exchange student you could study with?

> *I've studied languages pretty much my entire life: French since sixth grade, Spanish before that, and Chinese since my freshman year in high school. I want to stress the importance of learning languages before, during and after high school. Language learning has helped me decide a career path, a university path and really a life path. I now know that I want to do at least one or two, if not four or five, years abroad and absorb as much culture as I can get by being multi-lingual.* – **Ben Paulker**

Most competitive colleges look for applicants with four years of secondary school classwork in one language. If you have this, congratulations! (If you have this in more than one language, take a deep bow.) If you're not there yet, aim that way.

> *Going to a globally oriented college or university is key to having the right skills to land the job of the future. Make sure that there is a study abroad program that accepts credits for the courses you study while abroad and that the college has a study abroad office that will help you plan and set up course and housing arrangements.* – **Christy Brown**

GAP YEARS: A "gap year" is usually the period between completing high school and beginning college. Some students apply to college and defer for a year; others simply wait to apply. A gap year provides students with opportunities to:

- Gain global perspective early on.
- Build or shore **up language** skills.
- Develop maturity and independence.
- Participate in professional communities as a volunteer/employee.
- Pursue various interests to help define a career path.

Gap Years come in all shapes and sizes: participating in an organized Gap Year program, volunteering with a particular organization, teaching English abroad and even traveling the world as a tourist. Check out Admission Quest's extensive list of Gap Year programs.

When it's time to begin applying, consider choosing a college based partly on your language needs. Most colleges offer some sort of "global education," but all opportunities are not equal. No matter what career you're considering, language proficiencies matter to employers. Make sure before you matriculate that the institution will meet your personal and career goals when it comes to language learning.

Language can help anyone get ahead in any career, but I know from experience they are helpful even before then. The fact that I was taking more than one foreign language looked good on my college application, and knowledge of so-called critical languages, like Russian, is sought after. I feel that the number of languages and the length of time I have studied them was a factor in getting into my first choice college.
*– **Beth Cubanski***

*Looking back, learning languages was probably **the** most important part of my high school career. Whether it was using grammar in French to help understand grammar in English, or learning about other cultures because I wanted to travel to different countries, languages were a huge part of my learning process. In addition, I used my languages to help decide which university I wanted to attend. Most universities now require 3 years of a language. However, the top tier ones are starting to require four. I knew that I wanted a school with great domestic international program, and great study abroad programs as well. – **Ben Paulker***

As you search for the best undergraduate program, **ACTFL** encourages you to keep the following in mind. Before you apply to college, you should:

- *Check not only language offerings but levels as well. Why? Many universities offer majors in some languages but not others; languages like Chinese and Arabic may only be available at the introductory or intermediate levels.*
- *Check language offerings for alignment with your career interests. Why? If upper-level courses focus only on literature you may be limited in developing proficiency related to specific career interests; look for expanded language offerings that go beyond just literature.*
- *Check the availability of options to study abroad and how credits are transferred from study abroad programs. Why? A college or university that is preparing students to live and work in a global environment will encourage students to study and participate in international internships.*
- *Check Faculty backgrounds. Why? Faculty members should reflect many backgrounds and areas of expertise, not just literature.* – **Marty Abbott**

When you interview on campus, you should:

- *Ask about options for majoring in a language or double majoring in a language **and another** field. Why? The institution should encourage students to continue to develop language proficiency through double majors/minors.*
- *Ask about study abroad options and scholarships. Why? There should be a dedicated international study office with staff knowledgeable about scholarships.*
- *Ask about summer and academic year internships where you can use your language expertise. Why? The institution should make an effort to place students in situations where they are able to use their language skills.*
- *Ask about the number of adjunct instructors in the department and the role of teaching assistants. Why? Be wary of a significant number of adjunct instructors or too many courses taught by teaching assistants.*
- *Ask about Faculty involvement with students outside of class and extra-curricular activities of the language department. Why? There should be an active presence of the foreign language department on campus with guest lecture series, cultural activities, and service learning projects in the community.*
- *Ask about placement procedures and credit options for AP/IB and dual credit programs. Why? You should be placed appropriately in a language class so you don't waste time reviewing materials you have already mastered or sell yourself short by repeating coursework. The institution should also grant credits for college-level work completed in high school for Advanced Placement (AP), International Baccalaureate (IB) or dual credit programs.*

- *Ask about language-specific houses or floors where the language is spoken by the students. Why? Most language programs have a designated living space for majors and interested students where they are immersed in using the language. This is an excellent opportunity to accelerate the language acquisition process and improve your communication skills.*

- *Ask about resources for language students. Why? Institutions should have robust resources available to students in the target language from library holdings to magazines and videos.*

- *Ask to visit a language class and the language lab. Attending a class will give you important information about how language teaching is approached at the institution and how actively engaged the students are in the learning process. It will also let you speak with students involved in the language program.*

- *If you are interested in teaching at the K-12 level, ask if there is a program that prepares you for state certification to teach languages; ask to speak to seniors in the program or recent graduates. This is important if you want a teaching career; you should also ask about the student teaching experience to ensure teacher candidates are placed with highly qualified K-12 teachers.*

- *Ask about graduate programs and career services for students who major in languages or have high level language proficiency. Why? It's important to find out the track record of the Career Center in placing students in positions or graduate programs where they can use language talents. – **Marty Abbott***

Model United Nations (Model UN)

To expand your global horizons while still in high school, participate in **Model United Nations** (also **Model UN** or **MUN**), which is an academic simulation of the United Nations that aims to educate participants about current events, topics in international relations, diplomacy, and the United Nations. The participants role-play as diplomats representing a nation or NGO in a simulated session of an organ (committee) of the United Nations, such as the Security Council or the General Assembly. Participants research a country, take on roles as diplomats, investigate international issues, debate, deliberate, consult, and then develop solutions to world problems. More recently, simulation of other deliberative bodies, such as the United States National Security Council, has been included in Model United Nations, even if they are unrelated to the UN.

... if You're an Undergrad or Grad Student

To start anew or keep studying? That is the question. If you mastered French or Spanish in high school, now may be the time to start Arabic or Chinese. If you've studied one but haven't mastered it yet, don't switch. The merits of sticking with one language all the way through are great, unless you think it's not going to be particularly relevant. Many times switching can lead to no proficiency at all, and so work at mastering one. Above all, don't give the languages you've learned up – keep at it even if it's tough – it will pay off.

With campus life, your opportunities for formal and informal language study will expand considerably. In addition to classroom study, consider joining international clubs or language tables, regular tutoring swaps and cultural societies, or target language dorms. As your language skills improve, seek to read foreign-language newspapers and websites and listen to target-language broadcast media to keep up with goings-on in those countries where that language is spoken.

Find ways to immerse yourself in the language through study abroad, internships, volunteering abroad and immersion language courses. As you read the rest of this chapter, look for opportunities to incorporate language learning; they abound!

Globally-Oriented Coursework

Language is a great gateway, but not enough. Global employers seek graduates who have taken advantage of available coursework opportunities throughout their academic career to gain an international perspective. These include globally-oriented classes within your major, coursework focused on specific regions or cultures, courses that address broad global issues/globalization and classes on the global marketplace. Increasingly, top colleges are requiring international coursework (if not actual time abroad) for graduation. Whether your school requires it or not, you should demand it of yourself.

Globally-oriented Classes Within Your Major

Whatever your major, from business to history, literature to psychology, there should be classes available that explore the topic from a global rather than just a US perspective. Seek these classes out. They will broaden your horizons as well as looking good on your future global resume. In addition, they tend to be taught by multinational and internationalist faculty who can better direct you to readings and ideas that will help expand your world view.

Generally, it's best to take broad global or regional surveys –world literature, history of Europe, economics of African development – early in your academic career so as to get the 30,000-foot overview. You can specialize once you get a clearer picture of your own areas of interest. But if a great specialized course with a great teacher comes available early in your studies – the psychology of Hmong refugees, the history of Marxism in Peru, the environmental impact of mining in Australia – don't be afraid to take it. It may help define an interest.

Coursework Focused on Specific Regions or Cultures

To provide cross-disciplinary perspective, consider taking specialized coursework about that region/culture outside your own major. Are you a business major interested in China? Classes on Chinese language, history, literature and sociology will help you stand out. Do you aspire to a career in environmental issues in Africa? Courses in African history, population studies, art and comparative religion will give you a deeper perspective. Consider a minor in a specific area or regional study in addition to a major in a traditional discipline, or vice versa.

Courses that Address Broad Global Issues

More and more schools recognize that the interconnectedness of today's world requires a global and inter-disciplinary approach to understanding and addressing issues. In response, classes are being offered with titles like "the epidemiology of global pandemics," "the economics of cross-border financial crises," or "a communications-based approach to addressing global warming." Some schools are even offering global cross-disciplinary majors, such as "International and Area Studies," or "Global Business." These classes – and majors – are worth evaluating. Some may be too newly-minted to offer as much substance as more traditional classes, but others will be dynamite, and all will indicate cutting-edge global interest on your resume.

Classes in the Global Marketplace

We are all as affected by global business as we are by governments. Therefore, whatever your major, whether you think you'll work in business or not, I urge you to take at least a class or two that will help you gain perspective on – and demonstrate at least some understanding of – the way global business is done today. This is important even if you don't want to live overseas.

> *I'm pursuing a dual concentration in marketing and communications. My perspective on an international career is a little different because while I'm interested in pursuing a global career, I want to stay in the U.S, not move abroad. I realize that a global mindset is important and therefore I am learning as much as possible about international business, global branding and marketing solutions for organizations that operate around the world. When searching for a job, I'll emphasize my ability to work on diverse cross-cultural teams. And of course I'm willing to do some international travel, perhaps even move abroad for a few months because only through experiencing another culture can you truly understand it. Mostly, I plan to soak up as much international experience as possible while spending the majority of my time in the US – **Hailey Weiss***

What are your thoughts on working internationally but not moving abroad?

Expanding Your Global Awareness

For most people the undergraduate years are when they are most free to explore and experiment with new interests, tastes, styles and ideas. Take advantage of this opportunity to incorporate global and international experiences, whether that means traveling abroad or just exploring international resources on campus or in the community.

What do you do to expand your world view?

With global experiences are as close as your library or computer, there is no excuse for NOT developing global awareness. Try to:

- **Constantly build your global awareness.** Even as you seek out global coursework, stay in touch with the wider world by monitoring globally-oriented media, blogs, websites and other sources, real and virtual, as suggested in Chapter 1:
    1. Hone your cross-cultural skills.
    2. Pay attention to world events.
    3. Monitor business trends.
    4. Practice foreign languages.
    5. Monitor apps and blogs.
    6. Join local and virtual international clubs.
    7. Pay attention to hot regions and issues.
    8. Travel or study abroad.
    9. Seek a short-term job or volunteer abroad.

- **Take advantage of global groups on campus.** Most schools have globally-oriented organizations with names like the Asian Students' Union, Latin American Cultural Club, African Film Society or the European Student Investors. Sample a smorgasboard of groups early on, find which interest you, and get involved. They will help deepen your understanding of your chosen field and any regions/cultures you care about.

- **Reach out to community resources.** Beyond campus walls there may be immigrant associations, refugee outreach opportunities, cultural heritage societies or other resources that can not only continue your global education, but also help you keep a finger outside the academic bubble.

- **Enjoy global food, music, movies and art.** Instead of the usual pizza, try Indian food. Listen to the didgeridoo. Watch a film from Bosnia, or read the latest Shanghai murder mystery by Qiu Xiaolong. You'll expand your horizons, and may find areas of new interest. If nothing else, you'll have plenty of good answers when future recruiters ask "what got you interested in this area?"

- **Seek out international friends.** The best connections to other cultures are personal. When you befriend international students and people from other cultures you are building bridges for them and for you, bridges that are meaningful now and may prove useful for the future. Even relaxing to watch the ball game becomes a cross-cultural experience if you do it with your friend from Thailand. And your friend can take you deeper into his or her culture than you are capable of going on your own.

- **Travel abroad** on a personal vacation, and use the opportunity to learn. Travel isn't as mind-expanding as actually working abroad, but it can be educational and eye-opening, and can highlight your sense of adventure and appreciation for other cultures – especially if you visit lesser-traveled destinations in Asia, Africa and the Middle East. Consider also a "service vacation" through an organization like Volunteers Abroad or WWOOF. These often create deeper and more meaningful experiences than ordinary tourism, often at a lower cost, and look better on a resume.

I recently got back from spending two weeks in China and Thailand and the differences in culture were truly amazing. I hope to continue traveling abroad during my last year in business school and to take my career to an emerging market after I graduate. – **Caitlin Kappel**

What extracurricular experiences that you had as a student most inspired or helped you on your global adventure?

Going global in your extracurricular experiences will help enormously as you prepare for a global career.

Exchange/Study Abroad Programs

Studying abroad is increasingly important for many undergraduate degrees. Many MBA programs now make it mandatory. Just as American companies are sending more employees overseas, more American students are spending a portion of their studies abroad – an increase of approximately 10 percent every year for the past five years.

I regularly ask leaders of business and not-for-profit organizations about the importance of study abroad. Four of five agree that if all else between candidates were equal, they'd almost always choose the one with study abroad experience. – **Stacie Berdan**

Be aware that programs vary widely, from glorified vacations, to programs that take student self-sufficiency too far, like the one I reviewed that makes undergraduates find their own accommodations after landing, an intimidating prospect even for seasoned travelers. Some are academically rich, others mediocre. Some have rigid curricula, others are so loose even freshmen participate, beginning their college experience overseas (not generally recommended).

> *How have you balanced the need to study abroad and your budget?*

Assessments of study abroad programs vary widely. Googling "Are study abroad programs worth the money?" yields answers all over the map. I believe this reflects not disagreement on the value of time abroad, but tremendously uneven quality and value-for-money among programs. Carefully vet programs to ensure the substantial cost is worth it. Financial aid may be available, but often as loans, not grants. Carefully consider taking on what could be a crippling level of future debt in return for a program of uncertain value now.

A cousin once asked my financial guarantee on a $30,000 loan for a year at Oxford; the Don there said "ask anyone and you'll hear the value of having Oxford on your resume." So I asked; I called faculty I knew on Yale's graduate admissions committee. And I learned self-pay study abroad programs pull little weight at Yale: "all that tells me is the boy's parents could afford $30,000 to get Oxford on his resume." In the end my cousin did a much less expensive program elsewhere that ended up being much more academically impressive. – **Rebecca Weiner**

Studying abroad is undoubtedly fun and exciting. It should also be academically and culturally worthwhile. The programs you want will have solid reputations for academic rigor and cross-cultural outreach. They should require entrance testing, not be open to anyone who pays. Ideally, they will be integrated with your regular academic curriculum.

These are the programs that also will differentiate you on graduation, not mark you as someone who likes vacation cruises masquerading as study tours. Many programs now include intense cultural and intellectual preparation, research projects or presentations, or other signs of serious academic content. Top programs also may include:

- **Local language coursework.** Content classes (history, literature, business) taken in languages other than English show proficiency.

- **Diverse students.** Programs that attract attendees from all over the world will be richer culturally. They also foster cross-cultural teamwork, which helps to prepare you for global teams.

- **Regionally relevant content.** You should be going abroad to study in a particular geographic and cultural context. Ideally, your program will take advantage of this local access with introductions to area experts and enhanced access to local materials and perspectives, whether the topic is history, trade, regulation, literature, branding, engineering or environmental science.

- **Curricula-driven study abroad.** Some top programs today bring global students together to work on a regional problem, from water-use rights to fair-trade practices to cultural preservation. Employers know that time spent working on global teams in an academic context is excellent preparation for global jobs.

In sum, a good study abroad program will challenge, stretch, and enrich you. Such overseas stints have launched many a career because of the inherent curiosity, flexibility and interest in the world, which collectively helps enhance the student's:

- Cross-cultural awareness, which is critical to diverse global teams;
- Ability to bring global thinking to bear on complex issues;
- Language skills needed in a multi-polar world;
- Predisposition to and experience with global mobility

Finding a study abroad program where you live with a family and are able to use your language skills every day is so important. Consider taking on a conversation partner or language tutor on campus before you leave.

Often the language department can help you find someone. Consider staying abroad for the entire year if you can. – **Christy Brown**

What practical advice would you give students interested in studying abroad?

Proper planning will make or break any transfer you ever make overseas, and study abroad programs are no exception. Good preparation starts with an honest self-assessment as to what you hope to get out of a study abroad program. It continues with good cross-cultural training, and pre-reading about your new temporary home, from its language and economy to its public transportation systems. Your university or college should provide counseling that will help.

Determine If Studying Abroad is Right for You
From career objectives to course selections, you should be able to articulate the career benefits that will come from your time abroad. In addition, you need to be honest with yourself in determining if you have the right stuff for living and coping in a foreign environment.

Receive Cross-cultural Training that Encourages Problem-solving
Living in another country means figuring out how to take the local bus, order unfamiliar foods off of possibly incomprehensible menus and otherwise learning how to do common things differently than you have done them your whole life. This process will change you, stripping away your familiar habits and even self-identity and eventually replacing them with a more sophisticated international you. Good training programs can help accelerate this process by giving you a framework for:

- Understanding differences between/among cultures.
- Learning cross-cultural communications dos and don'ts.
- Developing skills to adapt to new environments.
- Working within diverse teams.
- Providing an overview of the cultural, historical, political and economic fundamentals of the host country.

Of course one-size does NOT fit all, and training can never cover every situation. But good preparation helps develop problem-solving techniques that can help you excel academically and live and work cross-culturally. In turn, you will enhance your career prospects and personal development.

> *Did your campus do anything to prepare you for your stint abroad?*

Choose a Location Wisely
Where you study abroad increasingly matters to prospective employers. If you studied in a country where you know the prospective employer has operations, you can work this into your resume or cover letter as appropriate. Branching out beyond traditional Western European countries and into high-growth markets like China, India or Brazil signals an enhanced awareness for growing global economies – and a direct link to the places most companies are expanding and growing (to hear a senior business leader's perspective on this, check out Perry Yeatman's video link in Chapter 6). These non-traditional destinations also offer more challenging situations, thereby intensifying the learning curve. And of course, if language acquisition is your focus, go where your target language is spoken on every street corner!

> *Where do you recommend students study abroad?*

Use Your Dollars Wisely
In a sluggish economy, schools and students often curtail study abroad programs. Seek to ensure the program you attend is both affordable and a good investment by:
- Pursuing destinations off the beaten path.
- Comparing program costs and going for no-frills options (which often involve home-stays and other experiences that immerse you more fully in the local culture).

- Opting for a short course. There are many different lengths of programs available, from a few weeks to a semester or year-long. The best incorporate intensive preparatory studies on the culture, history, language and economy of the country before you depart; many require independent research in-country and a presentation upon return. Predeparture discussions on culture, customs and current events can make the trip more enriching and less intimidating. Short-term experiences also offer a "taste" to students who are unsure if they want to spend an entire semester abroad. You can always return for longer later.
- Confirming, before departing, that academic credits can be transferred from overseas.
- Budgeting for currency fluctuations.
- Looking into work opportunities. If you can manage it with ongoing studies and local labor laws, working while studying provides a double-bonus: Influx of local currency and a dusting of gold to your resume: "worked abroad."

Do you have some financial tips to share for students studying abroad?

After you return home from a study abroad program, think about how your experience can be used to your advantage. How can you summarize and convey what you did and learned so that a hiring manager will appreciate it as a differentiating factor that is relevant to his or her business or industry.

Internships and Study/Work Opportunities

While most students tend to focus on study abroad opportunities, some of the most powerful preparation you can have for a future global career can come from an internship and/or short-term work experiences that you can arrange while you are still a student, either abroad – more typically – or in a globally-focused position at home. Whether it's a summer or a semester, there are plenty of real-life work opportunities waiting out there. As compared with studying abroad, internships and short term jobs offer:

- Real work experience, often in a low-stakes, low-pressure (and yes, fairly low-pay) environment. This lets you make inevitable "global newbie" mistakes with little pressure because of them. Having real work experience on your resume also gives you a leg up upon graduation, moving on from that low-pay entry-level job – or moving up and making it a springboard to a real career.

- Global experience for generally less money than study abroad programs cost. In many cases, the travel reimbursements and living stipends that internships and short-term jobs offer will let you break even and maybe even come home with a little left in your pocket, rather than a mountain of debt.

- The opportunity to stand out as a self-starter and a go-getter, able to think and work independently from a young age, as opposed to depending on nicely organized study-abroad programs.

I was fortunate to land an internship at the Embassy of France in Washington, D.C. There I spoke French on a daily basis, and I was able to interact with French expatriates and diplomats which served as a preview for upcoming cultural exchanges. Additionally, I participated in an independent study with a French professor, which culminated in a research paper written entirely in French. – **George Birman**

Interested in finding an internship before graduating? Here are some tips that also apply to finding a global job upon graduation:

<u>Do the Research</u>
Many companies, not-for-profit organizations and government agencies seek interns and short-term summer or term-time assistants or entry-level support. Some top places to look include TESOL for English-teaching jobs, the United Nations Internship Programme, AmericCorps, Vista and the Peace Corps. Many other international and multinational organizations offer opportunities as well, as do many corporations. There are even good meta-lists of websites that list

internship opportunities. Research what you will learn through the experience, and what jobs it will help you find.

Manage Expectations

Remember that these are internships and entry-level positions, so don't expect to get plum work. Keep your nose to the grindstone, doing whatever gets put in front of you well, and you'll find yourself moving up, maybe even getting a good job offer after graduation. As an entry-level professional, you need to be flexible when it comes to finances. For instance, consider applying in your home country and offering to pay your expenses in the target country if an organization offers you a job or internship and sponsors your visa.

Monitor Business Trends

Keep tabs on industries and companies expanding overseas, as well as foreign-owned companies in need of importing intellectual capital.

Develop Globally-focused Job-search Materials

Don't wait for graduation: turn to the global job-search fundamentals in Chapter 4 and start developing these materials now while your experiences are fresh in your mind.

Network, Network, Network

Network with professionals who have lived and worked abroad and get them to talk about their experience on campus on career days or as a guest lecturer. If you do a study abroad program during the spring term, network while you're in-country to try to find a job to stay on through the summer.

Global Degree Programs

Nationwide, schools are offering more globally-focused degree programs. Business schools have led the way as multi-national corporations (MNCs) need global workers. Companies with extensive international operations need of managers with extensive global skills. Significantly, companies now understand that they need a diverse leadership team with a comprehensive mix of skills, perspectives and experiences. Universities today offer degrees in global environmental studies, world trade, global epidemiology and other transnational disciplines. Whatever your field, there may well be a globally-focused degree available, and it can be well worth searching these out.

Carleen Kerttula, executive director of the MBA Roundtable, says 90% of members agree cultivating global mindset is a strategic priority.

Are there differences in the degree of global content across MBA programs? Absolutely! Young people seeking an MBA should carefully research programs and ask specifically what each school offers in terms of global opportunities. Programs that are more global will typically have a low percentage of students and faculty from any one geographic area, have campus or partnership locations on multiple continents, infuse global content across the full curriculum, have multiple language skills as a criteria for admission, and require one or multiple global trips or residencies as part of the program. – **Carleen Kertulla**

NYU Stern has done a fantastic job of encouraging students to think globally. As a board member of Stern's Women in Business club, I was an organizer of the annual conference, "Uniting Women Across Borders." We focused on the importance of traveling or working abroad. Working on the conference and interacting with people who worked in other countries has inspired me to try and do the same. – **Caitlin Kappel**

In the future, more programs will emulate the global-mindedness becoming standard in global MBA programs. Today's business schools appreciate that to compete, b-school students must practice in the global marketplace. Most top MBA programs now require mandatory time abroad, generally working on specific business problems or as an intern. Future managers learn to understand many organizational roles; they speak with customers, regulators and manufacturers. The very best programs include a pre-departure preparatory course covering culture, history, language, background and world economics. This is often followed by a research-based field trip, meetings with business, government and nonprofit leaders, a trip project and cultural activities.

Students cannot learn to do international business without having international business experience. All full-time MBA students at GWU participate in an international residency, which provides an interactive close-up with the complexities of the global economy.
*— **Dr. Liesel Riddle***

*Another telling statistic is the growing number of cross-continent MBA programs. The top-five ranked executive MBA programs (Financial Times, 2010) were all cross-continent programs, delivered most commonly via partnerships between leading business schools, e.g., the Columbia/London Business School EMBA. This was certainly not the case 10 years ago. — **Carleen Kertulla***

Do you think global degree programs properly prepare students?

The Bottom Line: Making the Most of Your Investment

Whatever global or other degree you pursue, it is up to you to be a discerning student, and make sure the substantial time and money you and your family will invest in it will be well spent. Colleges today are incredibly expensive and becoming more so each year, far outpacing inflation. A lot is at stake when you choose a college, courses and programs. If you're not careful, you could end up with $100,000 in student loan debt, only able to qualify for $25,000/year jobs. Nor does anyone want to put years into a degree only to find the courses you took didn't quite help you as much as you thought.

Choosing a School/Program with Solid Internationalist Credentials
There are many good sources for evaluating a school's academic caliber, from college counselors to the famous *US News and World Report* rankings to Bloomberg-Businessweek rankings of business programs, to college and university accreditation databases at the Department of Education. Use these resources. Research carefully.

When preparing for a global career, you want to attend a reputable school that also offers good global content, perspective and exposure. Here are some things to look for when choosing colleges or programs:

- Do they offer foreign languages? How many, which ones, and what are the language requirements for graduation?

- What study abroad/ global internship programs are offered? What pre-departure preparation is offered? What academic credit is available? What research work or presentation is required? Is coursework content taught in non-English languages?

- What percentage of the student body comes from abroad? What percentage of the faculty?

- What international or regional cultural clubs, associations or student groups are available on campus or in the local community?

- Are there any globally-focused degree programs or courses? How much regional or global coursework is required for graduation?

- What sorts of outside speakers come to campus? How many come from overseas and/or represent significant global organizations?

Once you find a suitably global program, you'll want to take full advantage of all the opportunities that the school offers to build your own personal globalist credentials.

1. Constantly build your global awareness.
2. Take advantage of global groups on campus.
3. Reach out to community resources.
4. Enjoy global food, music, movies and art.
5. Seek out international friends.
6. Travel abroad.

The Power of Minimizing Debt

Taken together, the school you choose and how you finance your education will determine how much debt you have when you graduate. That, in turn, will impact your flexibility. The more debt you have, the less flexibly you can pursue global opportunities here and abroad.

> *I have met many recent college graduates who had to turn down great opportunities in the media, the arts or the not-for-profit world – jobs or internships that truly interested them – simply because in their early to mid-twenties they had graduated from college with so much debt they couldn't afford to take anything but the highest-paying jobs available. How sad. Don't let it happen to you!* – **Stacie Berdan**

I worked part-time through my undergraduate years, lived off-campus in shared apartments, and cooked for myself. That let me earn my own room and board term-time, and focus my parents' contributions and my summer earnings on tuition. As a result, I graduated Yale nearly debt-free, and paid off the few student loans I did have within 6 months, leaving me free to do whatever I wanted. In the years after graduation I lived cheap, traveled the world and took a chance on some low-paying but exciting jobs abroad. The global experience I gained led to exciting – and high paying – jobs later. – **Rebecca Weiner**

Too many people walk blindly into the biggest-name admissions office that accepts them, and sign away on student loan notes without carefully considering their long-term impact. Here are some tips on minimizing debt:

- Carefully compare the student aid packages offered you, and don't be afraid to negotiate.
- If packages end up materially different even after negotiation, think carefully whether the smaller package at the bigger-name school is worth it.
- If your heart is set on a big-name school, consider going to a cheaper, local school for a year or two, and then transferring. That lets you graduate with the big-name degree, and less debt.
- Evaluate costs to determine whether dorms or off-campus life will be most cost-effective, and act accordingly.
- If you live off-campus, take roommates; if you share with international students, you'll reap a bonus in global exposure.
- Work part-time. You may party less than your classmates, but you'll graduate with a stronger resume and less debt.

Top Tips for Building International Qualifications

- Choose your college wisely.
- Apply for a passport if you don't already have one.
- Master your communication skills.
- Pursue foreign language intensely.
- Take globally-oriented coursework inside and outside your major including at least some business or global economics related classes.
- Expand your extracurricular horizons using the many cultural and global resources available on and off campus.
- Study and/or travel abroad.
- Seek a short-term job or internship abroad and/or in global affairs.
- Minimize debt as much as possible for future flexibility.

Chapter 4

Developing a Winning Global Job-search Toolkit: Resumes, Cover Letters and Elevator Pitches

Everyone talks about the all-important "elevator pitch." If you'd like to listen to mine, go to: http://youtu.be/S5o82fCO4Hk

YOU know you have talent and drive, but prospective bosses don't. You need to package, brand and sell your skills to prospective employers. Competition for good jobs today is tough and getting tougher, and employers know global assignments can be career launch pads. International employers want to know that you can succeed globally. To persuade them you can, you must show you have the skills and global awareness needed to succeed overseas. You must brand yourself as a global thinker and internationalist, which means taking a different approach to creating your global job-search toolkit:

1. International resume
2. Tailored cover letter
3. Elevator pitch

Your skills-based resume, great cover letter and concise and clear **elevator pitch** – a short summary used to quickly and simply define your career aspirations and relevant skills, between 30-90 seconds – must reflect global thinking.

Who Are You and What Are Your Skills?

Many people think domestic job search materials can just be tweaked for international positions. Not so. Global employers need to know your personal as well as professional abilities. Your ability to package your personal and professional skills and showcase your cross-cultural competence will be critical to landing that coveted first assignment.

What does cross-cultural competence mean to you?

Whatever materials you have – resume, draft cover letter, perhaps an elevator speech – put them aside for now. You may be able to reuse some of the material later, but don't make the mistake of adapting it. It's best to start anew, for the approach is quite different. The first order of business is to begin to think globally.

To put yourself in a global state of mind, watch, listen to and read world news. Pay attention to global events and international business trends. Open an atlas and study the countries in today's headlines, and read deeply on those that interest you. If you read a foreign language, check out online news sources in that language to get a better sense of what's going on. To keep tabs on global career news follow me on **Twitter**, friend me on **Facebook**, and connect with me on **Linkedin**.

> *You must pay attention to world events. You must follow media, like the Financial Times, New York Times, the Economist and the Wall Street Journal. Watch or listen to the BBC and National Public Radio (NPR). If you don't train your mind to think globally, you may find yourself going down dead ends on the road to launching your international career. –* ***Stacie Berdan***

What do you do to stay globally aware?

I recommend you begin the process of creating your international job-search fundamentals in the following order:

Define YOUR Global Brand. This is the first-step and a thinking exercise. What do you want? What skills do you have to help get there? Write answers down. The process will help you frame experiences, skills, personality traits and strong points in ways relevant to others.

Draft your elevator pitch. If someone asks in an elevator why they should hire you, what do you say? Write it down. Practice it. Learn to define your global professional self concisely, clearly, articulately and flexibly. What skills, values and interests can you offer that this firm needs? What in your resume is important for THIS global job?

Draft your cover letter. For this exercise to work, draft a real letter in response to a real job. You'll adapt your letter for actual applications, but use this first draft as a framework to help define the core goals and aspirations you seek to bring to your career. No generics!

Draft your resume. A good resume presents the skills and experiences that define you professionally. An international resume naturally does that, too. But it also illustrates your international education, experience and skills. And rather than organize the content around your professional experience, like a standard domestic resume, the international resume should center on your international skill set. Global employers need to not only understand what you can do – your technical skills – but also how well you will operate in a foreign environment. If this resume doesn't look significantly different from your standard one, you're doing something wrong.

Refine your social media bios. Don't forget about the importance of building your online brand through social networking sites. Although it can be a double-edged sword, employers expect to find you online, so make sure it's great.

Step 1: Define Your Global Brand

Too many people start out backwards – first writing resumes, drafting cover letters and applying for jobs, then trying to figure out who they are and what they really want. Instead, put the first job first. Who are you? What skills and personality traits do YOU bring to a global career? Everything else flows from understanding that.

Remember the quiz in Chapter 2? The answers to these types of questions help define the person you really are, and indicate your ability to do well in the international arena.

The Tough Part

Over the past two years, I have asked undergraduate and graduate students on many campuses what they feel is the toughest part of job search preparation. More than half say: "composing the elevator pitch." They admit having trouble defining and explaining exactly what they want to do in relation to the skills they have. Defining who we are in a sentence or two requires a challenging level of focus. We must mercilessly exclude anything irrelevant to stay focused.

What is the most difficult part of job search preparation?	
Writing the resume:	16%
Defining skills / elevator pitch:	53%
Tailoring cover letters:	28%
Applying online:	3%

Source: Go Global Survey 2011

The Process

It is imperative that you not skip or skimp on this process. The ability to craft a clear, concise self-description of professional and personal skills will make a remarkable difference in your success in the international job search process.

Goals

Let's get started. Make sure you have the time and space to devote to this challenging exercise. Ask yourself: What do I want in a job, a career, a life situation? Where do I want to be 5, 10 and 20 years from now? What career steps do I need to take to get there? Your answers can and will change over time, but it is important to lock in on accurate formulation now. This is, after all, where you are starting out.

Skills

Now consider your skills, interests, and values, both professional and personal. Ask yourself core questions: What are you good at? What motivates you? What do you like? Begin to make lists of the answers.

Take time for a reality check. What have peers or colleagues said about you? What attributes are you known for among your circle of friends or within your family? Ask mentors, teachers, colleagues, and friends you trust to review your list with you. Have you been honest about your strengths or downplayed weaknesses?

Links

Now it's time to create links between your list, and the attributes global companies need. Listen to what others have said about you and the connections to key attributes of globetrotters. Consider what you've learned from global experiences and how they contributed to who you are. Links common threads. What people, places or things have shaped your international perspective? Why?

What have you learned about yourself from your international experiences?

<u>Unify</u>

Now determine if you can group these attributes in ways that make sense and that are relevant to the personal and professional goals you have defined, be they business, cross-cultural awareness, management, leadership, organizational, technical or international. Begin to group words around each set of skills until you have a unified sentence or two for each group that you can now string together in a paragraph.

Through this exercise you will shed the robotic self-descriptions that often plague job-search materials, and move toward a colorful, rich biographical sketch that illustrates who you are and what you have to offer an employer. Now you're ready for the next step. You should have enough rich content to create a short marketing message about yourself: YOUR elevator pitch.

Step 2: Draft Your Elevator Pitch

If someone with the ability to hire you were to ask you in an elevator why they should – and you had less than a minute to answer – what would you say? As absurd as this proposition sounds, you'd be surprised how often something similar actually happens. Write it down. Then refine it by defining your global professional self concisely, clearly, articulately and flexibly. What skills, values and interests can you offer that this employer needs? What in your resume is important for THIS job?

A successful elevator pitch includes both hard skills (professional qualifications, education and language proficiency) and soft skills (personal attributes and interests that make you an excellent worker). These skills must speak to the global you. And even though your pitch is all about you, it's not only about you. First and foremost, it must be relevant to an employer.

Successful pitches are unique, catchy and brief. Use active verbs. Avoid adjectives and omit needless words. But remember – this is a professional description of YOU. You must feel comfortable saying it, which means it must be completely authentic and in your own words.

Now practice it over and over again until it flows naturally, which means not just that you have memorized it, but that you have incorporated it. And be prepared to use it – at a moment's notice. Here's an example from John Miles:

Hello, it's nice to meet you, I'm John Miles. It's funny you ask why I'm in London this week. I graduated last year from Duke's MBA program after spending eight years at Goldman Sachs in New York where I was a client relationship manager working with financial institutions in various business development roles as part of the firm's asset management build-out from 2000-2008. As a dual US/UK citizen, I decided recently to pursue opportunities here, specifically relationship management positions at growth capital focused private equity firms and diversified asset managers. As your company is one I've been targeting, would you have a recommended professional I can contact to discuss potential opportunities that may fit with my background?

I recommend that you write your elevator pitch first since it provides a framework for your cover letters and resume. It captures and communicates your best skills, and those most relevant and attractive to employers. Your elevator pitch will change over time as your experience increases and your desires change.

The Elevator Pitch
1. Describe yourself/your offering in clear, friendly words.
2. Focus on your outcomes for your audience.
3. Share how you overcame a specific challenge.
4. Give details of a happy ending and/or an immediate next step.

Step 3: Draft Your Cover Letter
Once your elevator pitch is complete, it will be much easier to write a cover letter, the one-page written summary used to catch an employer's eye. Cover letters are crucial. This is especially true in a global employment situation because your letter is the first impression a prospective employer often has of you.

Sending a bad cover letter is like showing up for work in dirty clothes or messy hair: it advertises slovenly lack of interest. Instead send a cover letter calculated to land you an interview. Excellent writing is a must and professional presentation critical so your international persona can come through clearly. Make sure you stand out, and radiate relevance to a particular job.

Employers craft job descriptions specifically to find the best candidates. Carefully read the job posting and choose requirements from the ad that you can meet. There should be nothing generic!

Checklist for Great Cover Letters

✓ *Professional tone*
✓ *Authentic*
✓ *Relevant to the job*
✓ *International infusion*
✓ *Excellent writing*
✓ *No typos*
✓ *No more than one page*

A good cover letter has three main components. This order is standard but not sacrosanct; you can be creative as long as you sound professional. In general, avoid sounding robotic and be careful not to use slang or make jokes. Each word, every sentence and each transition should be smooth. Together, the letter should impressively communicate your skills and dedication as well as why you are best for the job. Great writing does this. Allot time – hours if need be – to craft the best letter possible. If you can't say anything relevant to a specific job or company, you shouldn't be wasting your time or theirs applying.

In my 15 years of experience in the hiring manager's seat, I used cover letters to separate resumes into two piles. One pile was for those that contained something that caught my eye: an unusual or interesting opening, a relevant and unique skill or excellent writing style. The other pile I would put to the side because the cover letter didn't spark my interest enough: it seemed like a form letter, the applicant didn't really understand the job description or typos and errors jumped off the page at me. Unless some of those in the second pile had been flagged as particularly good by the HR department, I usually didn't read them. — **Stacie Berdan**

Introduction
Your introduction explains in a sentence or two how you came to learn of the company or job (with specifics, naming any personal referrals). Use the specific job title and the paper/website/bulletin board where it was posted.

---

eMail Correspondence

Don't fall victim to the common misconception that eMail communications don't matter. In fact, your email may be the first presentation of your professional self to an employer, so use it wisely. Although an email only introduces an attached cover letter and resume, it should not be colloquial but clear, concise, and grammatically correct with no typos. It should also be used as an opportunity to sell yourself. Use the subject line wisely, incorporating rich, relevant content.

The differences may be subtle, but they matter. Don't blow a potential job opportunity with sloppy email correspondence.

Body
Your body explains who you are and what you can offer. In it, you must clearly show how your work history and experiences demonstrate your ability to meet the job requirements. Let the employer know exactly why you can best meet their needs, preferably using their own words in a single, concise paragraph.

"The Ask"
Your "ask" asks for the job, or at least a chance to interview for it.

Step 4: Draft Your Resume(s)

International resumes capture professional, personal and international skills, as well as professional experience and education. Rather than being organized around your professional experience, the international resume is built around your skill set. Most people make the mistake of simply adapting a domestic resume – typically constructed around professional experience – and leaving out the most important part, the skills. But in international arena employers need to not only understand what you can do – your technical skills – but also your ability to operate in a foreign environment.

There are many great guides to resume-writing for the US market that offer useful basics, so read them. But you also need to go further, incorporating education, experience and aspirations that demonstrate you have the traits key to global success.

Drafting your international resume will be a lot easier if you have already completed the first three steps of:

Defining your career objective. Clear and concise description of what it is you want and the skills you have. Contextualize your experience, skills, personality traits and the things at which you excel.

Drafting your elevator pitch. This should include your hard skills, such as professional qualifications, education and language proficiency, and also soft skills, the personal attributes and specific interests that make you an excellent worker.

Drafting your cover letter. This builds on the elevator pitch in written form, explaining why your combination of skills and experience are right for a specific job. If you are tailoring a resume to a particular country, you may need to address specific requirements. Many people like to call the first section, "Career Objective," but I have found that many employers have evolved beyond this term. Instead, I prefer to use "Qualifications."

<u>Simplify the Flow</u>

Qualifications. The flow from your name at the top of the page to "Qualifications" builds a nice subtle bridge between the two as the reader is able to capture the essence of this person immediately.

Tips for Crafting Great Global Resumes
1. Simplify the flow: Qualifications > Education> Work Experience > Personal Data > Awards and Achievements. 2. Convey the most important information in the top one-third of the page. 3. Choose your words wisely: Use clear, concise and direct language. Use the active voice and action verbs to animate your accomplishments. Use terminology relevant to your field. Make every word count. 4. Incorporate cross-cultural aptitudes and international skills throughout, but without repetition. 5. Maintain a consistent format using bullets and short sentences, sequential information, dates, font style and size. 6. Proofread several times so as to eliminate all grammatical mistakes, spelling errors and typos.

That helps cut through the clutter with hiring managers who receive hundreds, perhaps thousands, of resumes every week. By using the "qualifications" approach, you can combine both your career objective and your professional, personal and international skills in a substantive, attention-grabbing manner right upfront.

"Qualifications" combines a career objective and 4-5 bulleted proof points that demonstrate your professional, personal, and global skills.

~~~~~~

SAMPLE:

Qualifications

Aspiring Account Coordinator who is innovative and highly organized with a global mindset and strong interest in starting a career in Technology PR with a global agency in China. Summary of qualifications include:

- Strong leadership skills; recognized by managers, professors and peers for effective work on teams
- Excellent communication skills; able to interact with people from different cultures as a result of studying and interning abroad in China.
- Enthusiasm for technology PR and first-hand experience in cloud-computing applications and social media tools in English and Chinese.
- Proficient in using Microsoft Office programs for research, data collection, analysis and presentation-focused projects
- Able to speak, read and write Chinese and English; loves to travel.

~~~~~~

Reflect each of these descriptive qualifications throughout your resume. For example, how did you acquire PR experience/where did you learn how to speak Chinese? Where did you work with those managers who recommend you?

Education. When first starting out in the job market, focus on your education, describing it as you would a job experience: list two or three points under your degree, detailing your interests, specific projects, study abroad, language learning, international clubs and awards. Stress anything in your experience that strengthened global awareness. Once you have significant job experience, your Education section will be reduced to degree, major, year and awards.

Work Experience/International Experience. If you're just launching your career, you won't have much professional experience to describe. That's only natural. But make whatever work you have done explicit on your resume. For each job, be sure to include accomplishments and relevant skills.

- Separate your professional from non-professional jobs and highlight the relevance of each to your qualifications.
- Group similar types of jobs if they were short-term (one year).
- Include skills in your job descriptions, as with qualifications.
- Indicate relevant international success factors.

Highlight your international experience in a separate section. Hiring managers scan through resumes quickly looking for relevant global experience, so make it easy for them to find. This section will market you as an internationalist and a global thinker and include:

- Foreign language skills and other cross-cultural exposure.
- Study abroad programs
- Internships and volunteer efforts abroad.
- International travel and courses.
- Experience with international clubs, organizations, non-profits.

But don't just write "speaks Arabic" or "studied abroad in Argentina" – bring it to life for the reader, for example:

- "Able to read and write Arabic, fluent in Egyptian Dialect; worked as volunteer news copy translator for Al Jazeera during the Egyptian uprising in February 2011."
- "Spent one semester at Universidad de Buenos Aires; this included two Spanish-only classes in history and literature, and work as an English tutor for UBA Outreach."

Your resume is an opportunity to showcase your skills, so do it with descriptive detail that highlights your achievements and demonstrates your ability to communicate.

Now that you have the framework down, fine-tune the content.

Convey the Most Important Information in the top third of the Page

Unless they are captivated, hiring managers don't read beyond the top one-third of the resume, so catch their eye, draw them in and keep them interested. That's why the flow from "Name" to "Qualifications" to professional and personal skills to education works. At this point they have a great sense of who you are and, hopefully, read further.

Choose words wisely

Your writing conveys your passion and your communication skills, as well as your experience.

Not-so-good:

"I want to work for a company in the aerospace industry because I have always liked the idea of flying. My father worked for Sikorsky, and I grew up with the idea that I would fly and would like to help others fly. I am especially interested in the new cooperation that exists between American aerospace companies and India, which is a big market for airplanes and other aerospace products today.

Much better:

"Growing up as the daughter of a senior Sikorsky engineer, I have dreamed since childhood of helping bring next-generation flight to the world. Today I seek to contribute to US participation in India's growing aircraft markets."

~~~~~~

Write long, then cut. Get ideas out, then pare fat. Keep only clear, concise, direct language that supports your goals and brand. Use the active voice – "I seek," "I managed," "I learned," NOT "I want to find," "I was given the opportunity to manage." Use action verbs to animate accomplishments – seek, aim, desire, manage, build. But many online resume searches use a formula that avoids verbs, so don't go overboard. Use terms relevant to your field. Make every word count.

Remember, you will likely end up with several resumes, each one tailored to a particular position or interest. Each should be adapted to reflect the keywords listed in specific job postings, and industry-specific language, as well as language common to companies or organizations in the field.

Incorporate Cross-cultural Aptitude/Global Skills Without Repetition
Cross-cultural aptitude includes intangible traits such as awareness, attitude, knowledge and skills. You must convince hiring managers that you understand and appreciate cultural differences, and can apply your knowledge in all your actions and behaviors.

International skills also include tangible competencies such as foreign language ability; training in cross-border functions such as international law, business or finance; or in-depth knowledge of or experience with a particular country, nationality or industry. These skills should be strongly highlighted in your resume.

> *Employers want professionals who exhibit cross-cultural awareness because they know it promotes clear communication, strengthens relationships, breaks down barriers, builds trust and leads to greater overall business success.* – **Stacie Berdan**

What examples do you use that effectively showcase cross-cultural awareness?

Maintain a Consistent Format
Consistency matters. You're spending significant time getting your framework and content just right, so put the same energy and attention into the formatting. Use short sentences and bullets to create a resume that is easy to scan. Use a standard font style and size for heading and content. Sequence your information from most recent to oldest.

Proofread
You may have the most interesting experiences and content included in your resume but if you have typos, it screams "sloppy, "careless," "disinterested." I don't know of any organizations that actively look for these characteristics. Make sure the impression you give on paper is perfect. Always print a hard copy to proof. Ask at least two, but ideally three or more people to review and critique your final version. Don't rush. Triple-check changes to ensure you've made them properly.

Step 5: Personal Branding Online
Digital and online capabilities have dramatically changed the way we work. That includes job searching. Although most employers still require a paper resume and cover letter, others are augmenting their review with online sources. Many professionals believe a simple

website address for an online resume or profile is all that will be necessary for job applications in the future.

Virtual Resumes

Virtual resumes can bring life to your one-dimensional paper version by adding examples, extensions and multi-media components that highlight your international experience and showcase your language skills. You can provide direct links to your presentations and projects, published work, photographs, references and blog or website. Virtual resumes provide employers with additional insight into your abilities, and help translate passion, experience and skills into marketable qualifications through multi-media.

You can pursue a few different avenues:

1. Create a virtual resume using a service, such as gigtide.com or Visual CV.com.
2. Create a professional profile on job sites, such as Jobster or Jobfox.
3. Launch your own website, either as your brand's online home, or specifically for job-hunting.

The first two have professional templates to follow and host sites. That simplifies getting started. But I recommend against hosting your materials on another's site; you'll want access to and control over content. So start a blog or web site of your own, keeping in mind that blogs must be updated regularly for freshness. Websites may offer a simpler way to post your job-search site materials.

> *About.me has become a popular means to present a unified personal brand online that consolidates various social media forms. I have a website, FB, Twitter and LinkedIn, but my About.me site is clean and simple; it allows me the opportunity to provide a snapshot of who I am — with an option for readers to find out more. – **Stacie Berdan***

Social Networks

Personal branding has become ubiquitous via social networking sites such as Facebook, Linkedin, Twitter, YouTube and flickr. Your profile and comments reflect who you are – your brand. Consider the role these tools can play in your job search. Use them to your advantage, by extending your international brand into your ongoing communications and following and commenting on international experts, topics, industries and places. But if you plan to use these tools for personal branding, be professional and don't let them become a liability because of compromising photos, rants or other unseemly content that you would not want a potential employer to read, view or otherwise be exposed to. It is impossible to know how many people have been denied jobs they otherwise would have gotten because of something on Facebook. The unfortunate reality is that a human resources person can do an online search and find out about your latest dorm party, and on the basis of that, decide you're not worth taking a chance on.

To help avoid such pitfalls, do a social media or Internet audit on yourself. What comes up when you Google your name? If there are some things you just don't want a prospective employer to see, work to eliminate them. If that can't be done, at least you can then plan a response to them if asked or come up with a strategy to increase your more positive stories to the top of the search list.

Remember that less can be more when using social networking for professional purposes – consider use of controlled lists, and careful screening of which list has access to which content.

Top Tips for Developing a Winning Job-search Tool-kit

- Think globally.
- Start from scratch; don't try to adapt materials designed for US job searches.
- Determine what you want and the skills you need to achieve it.
- Incorporate both professional and personal skills.
- Illustrate your cross-cultural aptitude through examples.
- Highlight your international skills as relevant to a particular job or industry.
- Use language effectively; keep your job-search materials focused and concise.
- Use social networking tools to advance your personal brand.

Chapter 5:
Pulling It All Together
Ready, Set...Go Global!

International careers come in all shapes and sizes. The Honorable Curtis S. Chin has moved between public and private sectors in the US and Asia, building a successful career. Listen to him tell his story on how his global career evolved: http://youtu.be/LN4KwxGQFqo

Now you're ready to start your search.

You understand that having a global mindset requires not only possessing the technical skills necessary for operating successfully in an international environment, but also the personal skills necessary for applying these effectively.

You know you must build your international credentials through experiences on-campus and off, including study, intern, volunteer or work abroad, foreign language pursuits, and international curricula.

You've learned how to create a winning global job-search toolkit by packaging and selling your skills to prospective employers with the right tools – and the right process.

Though preparation is more than half the battle, what remains is no piece of cake. You will need to prepare yourself mentally for a long, hard job search campaign. Landing your first international assignment will be among the toughest steps in your entire global journey because you are still unproven and will have to differentiate yourself to a global employer based solely on your background, interests and aptitudes.

You may be among the lucky few who land a great job after sending out just a few resumes; but don't count on it. Instead, anticipate a long process. Then you won't be disappointed, and you'll develop the persistence to get to success.

Today's tough economy makes the process harder than ever; you and I are not the only people who understand the value of a global job. Competition is fierce, and you may be competing against candidates with significantly more experience than you have. But if you prepare well, differentiate yourself carefully, and persevere, you will succeed.

*When asked "what is a good starting point for my career?" my advice is to consider the paths each job can lead to. Different jobs lead in different directions, some open many doors and some do not open many. Think of the network you will build on the job -- what kind of people will you work with? Who do they know and who would you have access to? For example: working at a big brand consulting firm, bank or blue chip organization means you will have the potential to develop a large network. A reputable well-known brand on your resume will mean it will be easier to get interviews. – **Jessica Austin***

Develop a Strategy and Action Plan

In order to launch an international career, you must have a strategy and a disciplined plan of action. You won't get where you want to go by hoping and waiting to see what comes along – you have to figure out what you want, and go in search of it. Your strategy should mirror the "elevator pitch" you have already devised. It should include:

- The type of job you are seeking.
- The geographic and/or cultural areas of greatest interest and in which you have the most extensive background.
- The general approaches you are taking to finding and applying for jobs.

Your strategic approach will depend largely on your field and your regional/cultural areas, but may include:

- Joining or attending meetings of professional or trade associations in your field.
- Reviewing and regularly reading trade journals, websites, conference reports, and the like to better understand what organizations are hiring and for what types of jobs.

- Joining or attending meetings of trade, business, cultural, scientific, educational, or other exchange organizations concerned with your regional or cultural area of interest.
- Setting up automated searches on websites and job boards that hire in your field and/or region, while remembering that often the best jobs are not advertised, but filled by word-of-mouth.

Since launching an international job search requires some global experience, be sure you spend time building up your qualifications before you start the job search. Throughout the journey, be conscious of the skills you are acquiring, both soft and hard skills – cross-cultural and technical. Periodically review your resume and other materials to make sure they are updated and reflect your latest acquisitions.

Your action plan should be a detailed, day-to-day tactical set of actions you are committing to undertake in search of the global career objectives laid out in your strategy. These should be what business strategists often call SMART actions: Specific, Measurable, Attainable, Realistic, and Timely.

Set up a schedule that you can commit to, one that will force you to conduct due diligence about who is hiring for what in your field and in the regions/cultural areas you are interested in. Leave no stone unturned. You never know where that one great lead will come from, but you'll maximize your chances of finding it if you open up as many simultaneous search channels as you can effectively manage.

Making and sticking to plans has value, but recognize that great leads and opportunities may come about serendipitously. International careers are built over time, often by pathways less linear and thus very different from traditional US-based career paths. For example, salary and title may be less important than experience and location. International careers capitalize on ever-changing global climate, with natural disasters and political uprisings often playing determining roles. You may begin with one objective, but end up somewhere completely different (but equally wonderful) as you learn about yourself. Flexibility is key to turning opportunities into stepping stones.

> *You never know where your path will lead, but that's one of the best things about working internationally: It opens up lots of doors. You decide which ones you go through.* – **Stacie Berdan**

Do Your Research

Make sure that in your action plan you assign yourself plenty of homework. As your job search progresses, you should do enough research to develop some real expertise regarding what organizations are hiring in your geographies and field, which ones are the most desirable employers, who you want to work for and why, and what you need to do to present yourself to them in the best light. This information will help you not just now but going forward as you parlay this first global job into a global career.

At a minimum, you should be able to answer the following:

- What are the growth areas in your chosen field (technically, and geographically)? What about those areas interests you, and how can you link your background and skills to them?

- Which are the best organizations to work for in your chosen field and region? What makes them stand out as employers? What are they looking for in employees? What areas are they hiring in?

- What specific locations do you most want to work in, and why?

> *I served two stints in the United States Government, once at Commerce and once in Treasury, and out of those experiences I was able to build on my private sector career. Whether you want to focus on the public sector, the private sector or the not-for-profit sector, in this increasingly interconnected world we can learn from different sectors. I always tell young people don't feel that if you begin with a career in the private sector, you'll always be there. Likewise when you're coming out of college and you want to join a great non-governmental organization or a trade association, it doesn't mean that one day you won't be working in business. Each has value to offer anyone's career.* – **Curtis S. Chin**

You can tell a lot about an organization by its website, annual report and news coverage. What do they offer employees? Look both entry-level and senior positions, checking for educational benefits and opportunities for global transfers. For instance, companies with global supply chains and international management on their boards undoubtedly have a brighter future than those trying to hold onto the last of their former territory in a single country. Another hint: if the executive board doesn't have much cultural, ethnic or gender diversity, it may not be as progressive in enabling global careers at other levels. Actively seek out companies that highlight working abroad as part of the corporate culture and value system.

As part of your ongoing research, you should:
1. Monitor business trends.
2. Pay attention to world events.
3. Explore public and not-for-profit sector opportunities.
4. Find out who the players are.
5. Follow your heart and interests.

Monitor Business Trends

Where do companies seem to be expanding? Contracting? Need help? What technologies are shifting in your chosen field? Are there major infrastructure shifts affecting jobs? Emerging markets and technologies change all the time. Which companies and not-for-profits are active in which parts of the world changes often. As you read about changing trends, constantly re-evaluate the skills you have that would benefit a company, a market or an industry, and go after jobs or companies relevant to those areas. Read newspapers; follow business and stock markets around the world to identify hot countries, industries, organizations, and opportunities.

What ethical issues do you think you'll face in working outside the US?

Pay Attention to World Events

Big global events result in a sudden explosion of specific opportunities. For instance, the lead-up to the 2008 Olympics in Beijing created a rapid expansion in business growth, cross-cultural exchanges and other career-building opportunities. The Olympics are taking place in London in 2012, Sochi, Russia in 2014, Rio de Janeiro in 2016 and South Korea in 2018 – have you thought what opportunities that might mean for you? Trade agreements and natural resource discoveries can lead to plenty of opportunity, as can political and cultural shifts and even natural disasters, and not just for journalists and relief workers. Just think of the law firms who began working decades-old property claims when the Berlin Wall fell, the telecom firms who benefitted when people in the Mid-East felt a need to stay in touch via Twitter, and the construction firms beginning to rebuild Japan after the tsunami. It's an ill wind that blows nobody any good, and if you're paying attention and able to respond quickly, even dismal developments may throw open career opportunities.

> *I spent almost every single school vacation and summer term at Yale traveling to developing countries around the world. I learned that billions of people lack access to standard medicine and infrastructure. I'm a biomedical engineer and designer in San Francisco working to empower communities in the developing world through practical solutions for major problems of poverty. I work to eradicate poverty by designing customized solutions to problems of access. I am committed to sustainable, scalable and affordable designs made with local materials. Human-centered engineering can create a future of abundance.* **–Elizabeth Marshman**

How has your global awareness driven your career objectives?

Explore Public and Not-for-profit Sector Opportunities
While job growth in the United States is typically driven by the private sector, don't ignore the wealth of global opportunities in the government/public service and not-for-profit sectors.

- **US State Department**: The best-known opportunities might be going overseas as a foreign service officer in the US State Department. And diplomatic service can be one of the most rewarding global careers.

- **Other US Government:** But when thinking of government, don't just think about the Foreign Service or the military. Consider being a CIA analyst, an FBI special agent or working for one of the Senate or House Committees on Foreign Relations. Even at state and city levels, there are global jobs. Many states have opened offices promoting exports, and Washington, D.C., offers up a range of associations focused on exports and business.

- **Non-governmental Organizations (NGOs):** There has been an explosion in **Rising NGO Requirements.** Today, leading global NGOs may offer intense career opportunities that rival the corporate world's in hours – and pay. "Wanting to do good" is no longer the only real job qualification. Honing and developing other global skills, from fluency in a foreign language to technical skills, such as engineering, accounting and law are a beneficial end result. NGO work over the past few years has evolved from ecology to democratization to microfinance. In fact, some experts argue that the NGO world has grown so fast it now has stature and credibility that rival those of the corporate world.

- **Foundations and Not-for-profit Organizations** Big and small, from the well-known such as The Ford Foundation, the Rockefeller Foundation, and Save the Children, to the very small such as Restoration Works International, NGOs are very much engaged in many projects and programs around the world.

- **Other International Organizations.** In an increasingly interconnected world, where business, government and the private sector would benefit from working together, there are many organizations, such as the ISIS Foundation that are very much focused on both what happens here and abroad. Whether it is telecommunications, healthcare or sustainable development, opportunities abound with such organizations.

- **United Nations Agencies.** There are also a range of United Nations agencies engaged in everything from women and children's issues such as UNICEF, to fighting corruption and drugs within the United Nations Office of Drugs & Crimes and addressing major health issues at The World Health Organization.

Many corporations now feature community relations, corporate social responsibility, compliance, corporate communications and other departments which support a range of good works. These departments seek to strengthen positive brand positioning for the organization. As a result, people involved with major NGO issues have the opportunity to move laterally from government, to corporations, to NGOs, and back again. There are many ways to "do well by doing good."

US Peace Corps

When US President John F. Kennedy launched the Peace Corps in 1961, it was open to virtually all Americans, including those with only a high school diploma. By contrast today, over 90% of Peace Corps positions require a bachelor's degree, with graduates with humanities degrees generally needing at least three months of teaching or tutoring experience to be considered. Similar "requirement inflation" has occurred with many NGOs.

More than ever before, business, government and the not-for-profit sectors are recognizing the importance of partnerships in areas of shared concerns. The results are new job opportunities for those willing to take the plunge, do things differently, and not be defined only by a search for profit or by a will to do good, but a combination of the two. – **Curtis S. Chin**

As the business, government, and NGO worlds come together, I urge everyone to study global markets. Even if you are sure you want not-for-profit work, you will be better prepared to help address environmental and other issues by understanding how markets work.

Find Out Who the Players Are

Some companies like to pretend they are more global than they really are. Use research to find out who is doing what. Read annual reports, pay attention to earnings and look for news on expansions, manufacturing growth or other signs of opportunity, here and abroad. Companies with global supply chains need global thinkers.

At the same time, be on the lookout for smaller companies based in emerging markets; many will be tomorrow's MNCs. Corporate dominance by MNCs based in developed nations is receding. In 2009, for instance, there was not a single Chinese company on Forbes' list of Top 25 global companies at all. This year there are four. Whereas the US and Japan used to dominate top global company lists, they have far fewer "candidates" this year and most likely, even fewer next year. Global job seekers must look beyond the top MNCs of the past, and track the rise of emerging companies around the world in countries like China, India, Brazil, Mexico and Russia, via resources like the Forbes map of the world's largest and fastest-growing companies.

> *Kraft Foods is actively looking for talent that understands foreign markets and consumer behaviors, as well as those who can succeed in cross-cultural teams. We cannot afford to be mindlessly global or hopelessly local. We must strike a balance, a concept we call 'glocal' in order to capitalize on growth potential of key markets around the world. – **Perry Yeatman***

Work with Your Campus Career Placement Center

Don't forget your campus guidance counselors! Many internationalists found their first overseas post through a campus career center. Set up a meeting with a counselor. The counselor can explain what global resources the Center offers, from lists of internships and job notices to subscription-based databases. Ask for guidelines to a logical planned path. Career counselors are trained to help you discover your skills and interests, so listen to their suggestions. They can direct you to some good starting points, and may well give you some insight into yourself.

Follow Your Heart and Interests

If there's a particular place in the world you love and have a connection to, find out which organizations are strong there. Your interest and passion will come through in interviews and in everything you do. It could make a big difference to employers.

Identify Markets, Industries and International Job Boards

So, how do you find jobs?

First, be prepared to go where the jobs are. If you're just looking for a stint in London, Paris or Rome – think again. The growth just isn't there. Moreover, with the advent of the EU and cross-border workers, there's even less need to import Americans, though if you have an EU passport that may help. For most people, most job opportunities will be in the key growth markets of China, India, Brazil, Russia, Eastern Europe and the Middle-East.

Emerging markets are growing at an average of 7-8% annually, down from previous double-digit annual growth. As a result, multinational companies are sending newly-minted graduates to these markets because of real advantages in flexibility and cost.

You still have choices about the type of local experience you want. You may prefer large, sophisticated cities, the thrill of the developing market, a country where you speak the language and/or political stability. Based on our survey, the following countries were listed as those with the hottest growth over the next few years.

Where do you think the greatest career opportunities are by country?

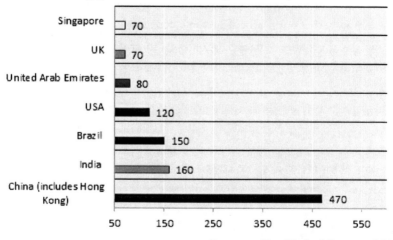

Source: Go Global Survey 2011

Spotlight on Brazil

The fifth most populous democracy in the world, Brazil sits on vast resources (including recently-discovered underwater oil reserves) and its industrial diversification is not tied to one field. For example, with a US exports just 2.5 percent of GNP, Brazil has not suffered due to US economic troubles. Brazil does struggle to meet its own growing demands for intellectual capital. Brazilian companies are some of the largest in the world, including Embraer, Vale and InBev/AmBev.

American students do well to focus on Brazil, learning Portuguese and international business on campus and visiting Brazil via study abroad programs and internerships. Brazil moved into the Top 20 rank last year at #19, an increase of 28 percent to 1,994 students, according to IIE's Open Doors Report. If American students are to be competitive in the international marketplace, campuses must be nimble and responsive to meet the growing demands of a booming economy such as Brazil's. Academic leaders should focus on Brazil and help students learn about this growing global economy.

> *There are several emerging multinational companies headquartered in Brazil looking to hire high-performing professionals to help them with international expansion and global competitiveness. A favorable exchange rate – which has seen the Brazilian Real strengthen against the US Dollar – means international talent is more affordable than it has been in a decade. Moving global talent into Brazil is now far less expensive than it used to be and thus far more appealing. –* ***Ramiro Prudencio***

~~~~~~

The China bandwagon, although still going strong, is now crowded. But there are still plenty of opportunities there for those with the right skills and temperament. For lots of information on dealing with this important global market see Chapter 7! Keep in mind that although some countries may be hotter than others, there are jobs everywhere – it's up to you to find them.

Spotlight on U.A.E.

The United Arab Emirates (UAE) is a federation of seven states formed in 1971 by the then Trucial States after independence from Britain. Since then, it has grown from a quiet backwater to a key economic center. Each state – Abu Dhabi, Dubai, Ajman, Fujairah, Ras al Khaimah, Sharjah and Umm al Qaiwain – maintains much independence, but a unified Supreme Council of Rulers made up of the seven emirs appoints the prime minister and the cabinet.

The UAE is one of the most liberal countries in the Gulf, with other cultures and beliefs generally tolerated. Its national language is Arabic and religion Islam. Oil and gas are major industries, and the people of the UAE generally enjoy a high standard of living.

Abu Dhabi is the capital, and the largest city is Dubai. Dubai now claims the world's tallest building, a rocket-shaped edifice that soars 2,717 feet and has views that reach 60 miles. The building opened in 2010 not long after Dubai came dangerously close to bankruptcy.

UAE is one of the fastest growing markets in the world. Those interested should visit, consider studying Arabic and learn about this cosmopolitan and energetic hub thriving in the Middle East.

UAE is a fascinating country with a unique opportunity. It has almost a blank canvas to work with and the ability to use learnings from other markets, as well as the means to build the best from the start. There is growth and energy here – the kind that has dwindled in the West – and young people are the majority. Due to the small native population, global talent will always be required: Talent with the desire to share knowledge gained abroad, the open-mindedness to adapt to the specific circumstances, and the creativity to find new ways to do things.

To get a foothold in this fast-growing region, students should consider studying or interning abroad to get a sense of the cosmopolitan culture and assess whether it's right for them. Gaining experience in another market that is saleable is key as UAE nationals are generally taken at the more junior levels. Once you have experience in diverse areas such as finance, industrial and hi-tech industries, there are plenty of opportunities to be had in one of the fastest growing markets in the world. – **Kate *Triggs***

Second, Focus on Growth Industries. Engineering, health care/pharmaceuticals, consumer products, energy and financial sectors are hot now, but these trends can shift. Keep your eye on stocks, media reports and industry indicators to figure out where the sustainable growth is. Following a range of credible news will help you sort fact from fiction and short-term blips from long-term trends.

> *My business is global; 75% of my sales are outside the US So it's frankly just not possible to have a US career any more. If you want to grow and expand into senior leadership, you've got to be thinking beyond the borders. You've got to go global.* – **Diane Gulyas**

Which sectors are growing the fastest globally?

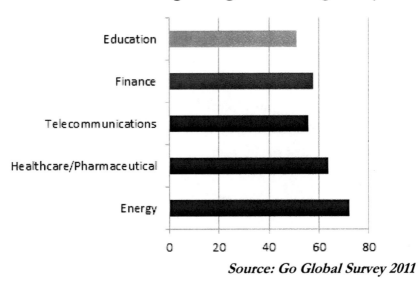

Source: Go Global Survey 2011

Which countries and industries do you think offer the greatest opportunities?

Network - Network - Network

Network is both a noun and a verb, and although everyone always tells you to network (verb), you should begin by recognizing and assessing that you are already part of a network (noun) whether you know it or not. To determine your current network, think about the groups you belong to or are associated with, and think strategically about the overlaps with these groups and your aspirations. Consider school (college alumni), faith-based, community, summer job, and club networks. Don't forget about family and friends!

Networking is one of the most important aspects of career success. Tell as many people as possible about your global aspirations. Network EVERYWHERE. Ask everyone you know – or who knows your work – for contacts they may have at your target companies and/or in your target countries. Then email contacts to ask about opportunities. Seek contacts from family, friends, professors, and organizations, trying for as much advice as you can from professionals in the "real" world. Things are changing fast, so stay in the loop. Join professional associations and clubs and network, network, network. **Find a mentor** who can help you negotiate securing a foreign assignment and who can be an advocate for you. To structure your approach:

- Build an organized list of contacts on email.
- Request to connect with professionals on LinkedIn.
- Follow up with people you've met, asking for one piece of advice, an introduction or an informational interview.
- Do not be afraid to ask for help of anyone you think can help.
- Make friends when you travel.
- Join local language clubs and participate in cross-cultural opportunities and activities.
- Attend relevant conferences on campus and off.

It's important to keep your networking communications short, simple and not burdensome, since most people are connected 24/7 and busy. Stay focused, never write more than a paragraph or two and always send a thank you note with an offer to return the favor, either to the person who helped you or others they may know.

Do you have networking tips to share?

Interviews: Prepare Properly and Execute Flawlessly

Finally! You've been invited to an interview. Now it's time to bring it all together by presenting all the qualifications you have painstakingly gathered in a way that will motivate this employer to hire you.

The interview is the moment of truth in your job search, where a hiring manager determines whether you're the individual he or she is looking for. Are you qualified? Do your skills match with the job? Do you have the characteristics necessary to succeed in the position? Is there something that differentiates you from the competition?

Questions Most Often Asked in Interviews for Global Jobs	
Why do you want to pursue an international career?	85%
Give me an example of your cross-cultural competence.	66%
Have you ever worked/interned abroad?	63%
Are you fluent in more than one language?	52%
Have you studied abroad?	42%

Source: Go Global Survey 2011

Based on research conducted with hundreds of globe-trotting professionals over the years, a few qualities rise to the top as critical in the interview process. These qualities are as important to the job seeker as they are to the hired employee. If you exhibit these during your interview process (and, in fact, throughout the application process), you will differentiate yourself from others:

- **Be determined and persistent.** Don't give up, don't be dismayed, follow your dreams but be practical.
- **Present a confident person with strong sense of self.** Passion and drive come through in a confident person.
- **Be innovative and willing to take risks.** You must be willing to go the extra mile, and figure out new ways when the old ways don't work. You will do this in the search and on the ground.

- **Show excellent communication skills.** From writing your cover letter and resume to presenting your qualifications in face-to-face meetings, your communications skills will be appraised. You must clearly communicate your technical skills AND your soft skills, especially those that will enable you to work well across cultures.

- **Gather intelligence.** Make sure you scour the organization's website – following up if possible with a contact you have there – and adapt your talking points to reflect the language and mission of the organization.

- **Practice!** You must prepare and practice your messages – HOW your global perspective will make you an ideal employee. You must be able to make the connections clearly and concisely between your skills and work experience and the position. Practice your pitch by yourself so it flows smoothly, then practice it with a friend or colleague. Also practice your greetings, how you'll sit down, where you'll look (in their eyes), how you'll smile. Even practice the telephone call, for that's part of the interview, too.

One particular warning: You may interview with someone who does not respect, appreciate, or understand the value of your international experience – or they may not find your experience impressive. There are plenty of people out there – I run into them almost every day. Learn how to spot this and then bridge to your other relevant experience beyond the international.

My coaching is designed to make a strong, positive impression during every step of the job-search process: developing an effective self-pitch, building a network, completing applications, interviews, and negotiations. Most of my clients have been successful because they:

1. *Identified their USPs "Unique Selling Points," meaning, what do they have to offer that is UNIQUE and NEEDED in today's market?"*
2. *Identified a new field of interest. If there is no overlap, or they do not enjoy doing the type of work that demands their unique skillset, they identified a new field of interest they are passionate about and educated themselves in this field. Most obtained a new degree or certification.*

3. *Developed an effective resume/CV and understanding of the application process.*
4. *Leveraged their network, expressing genuine interest in others and doing things for others along the way (people help people who help them).*
5. *Networked. Attended networking events to meet new people and practice delivering their brief and interesting self-pitch until they could deliver it confidently, be authentic, and sound passionate about it.*
6. *Followed up with people soon afterwards: LinkIn with connections and post professional career-related updates to stay in their radar. Make invitation and thank-you emails personal-refer to meetings or work.*
7. *Learned from the process. Learned and practiced interview techniques, wrote cover letters customized for each job, and took set-backs during the job application process as learning opportunities to improve the next time. Sound straightforward? It is not. Most people find it very difficult to navigate today's job market and find themselves experiencing fear, depression, and even hostility during their job search. –* **Jessica Austin**

Be Flexible in Your Interview Style.

The world is filled with diversity and that is true for hiring managers as well. Managers and interviewees each have their own personal interviewing style, and it's important to recognize this. Some treat the interview casually, while others are stiff and ask specific questions. It's up to you to try to figure out the interviewer's style and how best to incorporate your messages into your answers in light of that style.

International job interviews often throw people off with personal questioning. Candidates for global jobs are more likely than domestic candidates to get asked about family, health, and other factors that may affect an international move. If you are married, you may be asked how strong your marriage is, and whether your spouse knows you're applying for jobs overseas. Interviewers may probe to check you really understand what it's like to live, work, or travel globally. Sending you abroad is a big investment, one they want to be sure will pay off –that you won't end your term early or give up due to the hardships global workers encounter. They may require psychological tests.

Highlight Your Ability to Work on Virtual, Global Teams

Such teams are increasingly commonplace in the workplace today and the odds of your working on a virtual, global team – with members on several continents, speaking multiple languages, covering chaotic time zones – are great. Even small companies are going virtual these days. Yet people don't follow basic guidelines for cross-cultural success. Understanding and proactively managing cross-cultural differences can be a strong competitive advantage, so be prepared to showcase your ability to work virtually and to showcase your cross-cultural awareness.

How have you handled working on a virtual team?

Push On, Yet Manage Your Expectations

You should be prepared to be persistent for months in your job-search, but also be prepared to "leave tomorrow" if a great job comes up; hiring decisions for global positions are sometimes made very quickly. The instability can be maddening, but it's part of the process – most international jobs have more than their fair share of instability.

> *While the immediate value of taking a job overseas appeared negative when I accepted the assignment, the future value was enormous. The financial gains I have made since as a result of the experience far outweighed any short term pain! It's an investment you must make in yourself to compete in the future marketplace.* – **Sharon Knight**

Don't Try to Make the Discussion Be All About You

Your job search cannot be all about your own global experience and desire to move to Mexico or South Africa. The interviewer must walk away knowing what you can do for the company, and how you can help drive performance. Make your case. It pays off.

Don't Be Too Greedy In an Entry-level Job Interview

Although a great expat package is very fine indeed, even experienced managers don't seem to be getting them much these days, unless they are very senior, being sent to "hardship posts" or have some rare or stellar skill. These great packages have become rare for two reasons: 1)

104

companies need more international workers and so must send more and keep costs down; and 2) companies know employees need global experience, so global jobs are more competitive than before.

Manage Expectations About How Soon You Will Be Sent Abroad

If you want to go overseas immediately you may need to consider heading off without a job, then seeing what turns up on the ground. More companies are open to hiring Americans as "local hires" in emerging markets – remember when I said new grads are eager and "cheap." That can be a great adventure, but it's not for everyone.

Be Prepared to Work Domestically for a Few Years

Some companies may want to test your mettle at home in a safer market before they send you abroad. That can be to your benefit, leading to more senior postings down the line. But how far down the line, and what will you do in the meantime? When you interview, examine the situation and determine if there are realistic global opportunities a few years down the road. Be open to possibilities. Maybe you can wait to go overseas, can get in the door now, perform well, and keep eyes and ears open for opportunities. Once inside, you will have advance notice of emerging prospects and the inside track.

Persevere

Contact employers regularly, not just to find out who is proactively hiring, but to enquire where your services may be needed, and when. Don't give up: follow up regularly with contacts; keep looking elsewhere (even when you have a tentative offer); and keep adding related international experiences to your dossier.

Top Tips for the Job Search

- Develop a strategy that features a disciplined plan of action.
- Gather intelligence. Do your research.
- Work with your campus career placement center or an international career coach.
- Identify targets and network.
- Look for trends.
- Connect the dots between your skills and an organization's needs.
- Prepare properly for the interview.
- Persevere yet manage expectations.

Chapter 6

Launching an International Career

You've learned a lot along the way so far and, perhaps, one of the things you've learned is that you want to make a difference in the world. That's what Elizabeth Marshman decided after she graduated from Yale. She set up a not-for-profit organization, ReEnvision Design, and has set her goals on eradicating global poverty: http://www.youtube.com/watch?v=AYHrWOfXJf4

Whether you want to start your own venture or seek a position at an organization, landing your first international assignment will be among the toughest steps on your global journey. You're still unproven and will have to differentiate yourself to a global employer/ financial backers based on your background, interests and aptitudes.

But you've persevered, and found that international job. Whether it's a 3-month assignment, international transfer or as a member of a global team, congratulations! This section will help you make the most of that first job as a springboard to a global career.

Your first year on the job is critical. Do everything you can to make the most of your experience, whether you've moved abroad or are working in an international position in your home country. Doing your best every day forces you to figure out what it takes to succeed in ways that a traditional entry-level job might not. Build and nurture your network. Working as part of a global team takes commitment, fortitude, and a great deal of energy. You face a steep learning curve, but knowing that going in will help. You also know that the challenges you face on the global path you are on will fast-track your career.

Before we move into specific country advice, here are a few quick tips to keep in mind as you make the move.

Listen Carefully

One of the best ways to ensure success in the global workplace is to listen carefully so as to figure out what's going on and why. Only then can you begin to make a difference. Pay attention for the first few months, while keeping your head down and doing the jobs assigned to you as best you can. Meantime you can thoughtfully consider what – if anything – should be changed in your work environment, and whether you should act on those changes or not.

Things are not always as they seem. Be cautious and take notes. Ask for advice. Learn the written and unwritten rules, which may vary by industry, hierarchy and culture. Pay attention, ask questions, and figure out how things are done in this new landscape.

Don't Be Too Hard on Yourself.

Cultural mistakes and bungling are part and parcel of the international experience. As the old saying goes, the only way to never make a mistake is to never do anything at all. So be gentle on yourself, and try to be understanding when others goof up, too. If you don't already know how to laugh at yourself and your mistakes, get used to it! Don't hesitate to use gentle humor publicly (especially about yourself), as it can dissolve cultural walls quickly.

At the same time, try to learn from each of your mistakes (and from those you see others making), so that you don't make the same ones over and over. Never fear – there will be plenty of new mistakes to make as you continue to try new things. Unconditional acceptance is one of the most important requirements of a truly successful experience abroad. You have to let your barriers fall and accept new ways of interaction, new ways of thinking, and new ways of living. Only then will you begin to understand that our world is indeed a very large and complicated place, with countless paths to countless ends. As

C.W. Metcalfe and Roma Felible put it in their classic book, *Lighten Up! Survival Skills for People Under Pressure,* you need to "escape from the center of your own universe."

Romance/Dating

In our ever-smaller and more interconnected world, cross-cultural dating is becoming more common, in many different contexts. If you Google "advice on cross-cultural dating" you'll find hundreds of sites and ideas, many not worth the bytes they take up on the blogosphere, but others offering some real gems.

Keep a Positive Attitude

You are about to embark on one of the most exciting journeys of your lifetime. Along with the excitement, however, will come inevitable challenges. You should know going in that some days will be dark and difficult. Do your best to keep a positive attitude by figuring out, early on what refills your tank, and buoys you up.

> *Take care of yourself, eat well, exercise, get plenty of sleep. Living in a completely different country and everything being so "new" can take a toll on you mentally and physically. So eat healthy and stay active, maybe even incorporate a new activity. I enrolled in tai chi classes, a form of martial arts, and while I was initially a bit hesitant, I'm really glad I did it. It was a fun way to exercise and a great opportunity to learn something unique to the culture. –* ***Kelly Loughlin***

Make Friends and Connections

One of the greatest benefits of an international career is meeting new people from diverse backgrounds. You'll learn from them and they you, but you will learn much more if you are in their country. Recognize, though, that many cultures don't let outsiders in right away. It takes time and effort to keep an open mind, and to reach out and make friends cross-culturally. You have to keep your ethnocentrism under control; if you go overseas or work in a cross-cultural environment YOU will likely be the different one, the strange one, the foreign one – not the hundreds of people around you. Build relationships with local friends, don't just stick to people "like you." At first you may seek out primarily a local mentor, or cultural guide. If you express genuine interest in and respect for their culture, you're on your way to becoming friends. Focus slowly on building relationships with everyone you meet; you'll begin to integrate and to be part of the fabric of your new home.

> *Studying abroad and interning at an Investment Firm in Dublin gave me the essential fundamentals to prepare myself for the quickly evolving global economy. It also helped develop the skills needed to be at the top of my competition in my job search for post-graduation. I attribute my international experience along with other internships to landing a position at one of the top financial training programs in the world, in one of the largest global companies in the world.* – **Matt Conway**

Do What It Takes

Even as you experience the double newness of your new job and new environment, you should also begin preparing for your next move, even if it's not in the near-term. This means doing superior work at your current job so your bosses will want to promote you, while also paying attention to any opportunities that come along that can parlay this experience into your next job. Some key tips for turning your current job into your next step up the ladder include:

- **Do whatever work is assigned to you as well as you can.** This will help bring you to the attention of senior managers, and earn you more challenging and interesting assignments jobs over time.

- **Find a mentor – or three.** Begin to identify the people who are leaders in your company and/or field, and seek opportunities to work with and learn from them, both formally and informally.

- **Volunteer for the extra assignments.** Be the one who delivers despite the odds of time zones, cross-cultural virtual teams, or language barriers; the one who thinks "what do we need to accomplish today" instead of "when can I get out of here."

- **Share the glory.** No one likes a braggart. If your hard work brings success, tell anyone who asks that it was a team effort, and/or that you owe it all to great leadership. Send out that group email thanking everyone on the team for a job well done. Over time, everyone from your colleagues to senior management will notice both that all the teams you work on flourish AND that you demonstrate good leadership skills by not hogging all the credit.

- **Get to work early.** Those old sayings about early birds getting the worms are true. Getting to work early makes you more productive, and is a reliable way to catch the eye of senior managers.
- **Begin to package your success.** While demonstrating good manners and leadership, use emails to help document your own success. Save them, along with any thank-you notes or positive reviews from bosses, colleagues or clients. Continue to refine your "elevator pitch," to reflect your growing skill set. Quantify and qualify your successes succinctly. Enlist allies to help as needed. When opportunity knocks, you'll be ready.

Some Important Messages You'll Want to Watch

Before we wrap up and move on to the specifics of China, I'd like to share more multi-media stories. These globetrotters each have messages to share; find the links on my website and watch them all!

Constance deNazelle, student, talks about the importance of her international experience and how it plays into her career objectives.
Allison Frick, young professional, tells her tale of how she combined journalism with Spanish-language degrees to pursue a bilingual career.
Diane Gulyas, seasoned international business leader, talks about the importance and necessity of international travel in leading a global business today.
Perry Yeatman, author, internationalist and business leader, talks about the importance of pursuing an international career in developing markets.

Travel, Have Fun – Enjoy Yourself!

One of the most enriching aspects of a global career is the opportunity to explore. Take advantage of traveling or being overseas to enjoy the local culture and regional attractions. Living in another country provides vast possibilities for adventure. The world is a big place and there's so much to see. Don't waste time, and spend money wisely. You don't have to travel first class to explore the world; in fact often the more like a local you travel, the better. When you have business trips, take an extra day to get to know your destination. That will be personally enriching, and also expand your professional expertise.

To sum up: remember that working overseas is a rich experience. Go global not just for work – it's a rich personal experience, too. You'll grow immensely. You will change, and the world won't look quite the same to you after. As one friend often says to me, "Our heads just aren't screwed on the same way anymore." Working internationally can be one of the most rewarding experiences of your life. But no global assignment will ever be a bed of roses. Even the most seasoned foreign traveler faces disorienting culture shock with each new assignment. Simple everyday actions like going to the grocery store can be a challenge in a foreign environment. There may be confusion over roles, embarrassments with language, homesickness for loved ones left behind. There may be financial challenges, whether you take a job as an in-country "local hire" or as an expatriate. Your tax return alone may turn into a 4-inch high stack of paper.

But your global assignment will also give you an unparalleled opportunity to expand your worldview as you learn about other peoples and ways of lives … to acquire treasures you never imagined owning … to deliver results for your organization in a strange land because you have overcome differences in language, culture, regulation, labor laws, sourcing issues, regional economics, laws and politics – all at the same time!

You'll build your self-confidence as you deal with all these issues and more … and pile up responsibilities and accomplishments you never would have stateside. It's a tough job, but working internationally can be one of the most rewarding experiences in – and best ways to launch and/or fast-track – your professional career.

Chapter 7

Navigating the Pathways To China

By Rebecca Weiner

China is truly an amazing land of career opportunity today. Check out this photo essay by Robert Fried, founder of the Chinese language Language Institute: His rise from student to teacher to entrepreneur-owner of a chain of language schools, at the speed with which he accomplished it, would be hard to imagine in the US today, but is just part of the territory in China:

http://www.youtube.com/watch?v=9vp6E6fbx48

China and the China trade are full of opportunities for enterprising Americans. This chapter will help you understand what China does – and doesn't – offer, and how to make the most of those opportunities. I wrote this chapter based on 27 years of experience with China and China business, and also based on interviews and correspondence with people from around the world, young and old, who are pursuing great careers in and involving China. You will meet many of them in this chapter. I hope through their stories and mine you will gain ideas, tools and inspiration to find a "pathway to China" that makes sense for your own career and life goals.

The New China Gold Rush

Long ago, in a geo-political universe far from today's, Americans learning Asian languages were taught how to speak to servants. Chinese and Japanese language textbooks of the 1940s and 1950s were full of phrases like "please have supper ready by 6:00," and "be sure to change the sheets in the guest room."

Times have changed. Consider this recent Yahoo Group posting to the international community at Yale University:

"I am looking for a teacher of Chinese language for my 12 year old (English speaking) son. I can barter cleaning services."

Today, at least one American is already offering to clean houses for Chinese people in exchange for access to language and cultural skills seen as important for her child's future. This sign of the times is likely just the beginning.

As China's economy has boomed while America's has teetered and faltered its way out of the Great Recession, China has become a major new destination for job-seeking Americans. The media have commented widely; almost every day offers a new perspective on China, including China-bound Americans as part of a larger trend toward job-seeking overseas.

There's good reason for fascination with China. China's economic boom, launched in 1978 by the "period of openness and reform" that swept away the destructive late-Maoist policies of the Cultural Revolution, has continued almost unabated ever since. For 33 years, China's growth rate has waxed, waning only occasionally and moderately. The 1997 Asian financial crisis, swine flu epidemics, earthquakes, tsunamis, and the 2008 global recession crushed other economies; China's merely modulated, perhaps dipping from 11% to "just" 8% annual growth – while growth rates in developed economies like the US and Japan hovered at 1%, or turned negative.

As a result, since 1978, China has risen from a bit player in the global economy to ruling much of center stage. In 2010 China surged past Japan to become the world's second largest economy. Many economists predict China will surpass the US by 2020. And despite much fretting about China's debt levels and economic bubbles, investment is still pouring in, enough so that China may well continue to achieve "soft landings," avoid hard collapses and maintain rapid growth well into the future.

All this may seem frightening to Americans. Certainly China's rise is already affecting American life. Her hunger for raw materials has helped fuel recent global price rises for everything from gasoline to steel. Her factories have long sucked in global manufacturing jobs, and her skilled engineers, architects and other professionals are increasingly pulling higher-end jobs from America and other countries. In just one famous example, the networking company 3Com adopted a "China out" strategy, moving their CEO seat to China along with 4,000 of the company's 6,000 global engineering jobs, most staffed by Chinese (word is, 3Com's China prowess was a key driver of their recent merger with HP).

Change is always scary, but it is also inevitable. Nothing lasts forever, including US global dominance. Arguably, like England, the former Roman Empire we now call Italy, and many other nations (including China herself), the US may find that stepping down for a time from the role of sole super-power and "top global cop" may, in fact, eventually ease stresses and improve standards of living at home.

Meantime, periods of transition are always ripe with opportunity for people ready to respond flexibly to changing needs. The shifting power balance and trade and economic relationships between China and the US offer massive job opportunities for Americans willing to learn about and travel to and/or work in China.

One note: it is beyond the scope of this chapter to delve into the moral complexities of Americans working in China or for Chinese firms when China's power is growing while she does not share all US values. Good groups to turn to for balanced insight on those issues include Duihua, the National Committee on United States-China Relations, the China Law Center at Yale, the China Rule of Law Initiative at the ABA, the China Environment Forum, the media initiative of the Council on Foreign Relations and the ICO. There is also excellent insight on China from people like James Fallows in the

Atlantic, and books like Fred Bergsten's *China's Rise,* Robert Rotberg's *China into Africa,* Susan L. Shirk's *China: Fragile Superpower* and David M. Lampton's *The Three Faces of Chinese Power.* For my personal opinions on some China complexities, please see the Tikkun website (where I have posted pieces on Wal-Mart and Chinese labor laws and on the Falungong), and a book I coauthored, *Culture Shock! China: A Survival Guide on Customs and Etiquette.* Here I will say only that I believe deeply that Americans involved with China have far better opportunities to help shape China's relationships with its own people and those of the world than do those who sit on the sidelines pointing fingers.

> *In my years in Hong Kong I grew so much professionally and personally. I loved my time there, and also sometimes desperately wanted to escape – the love-hate relationship typical of many expat experiences. I was working in Hong Kong throughout the lead-in and follow-on to the British handover to China in 1997, and came to deeply understand the feelings of local people. There were torrential rains, and the local saying then was "the victims of the Tiananmen Massacre are crying for the people of Hong Kong." My team was confused, struggling with issues from language (their native Cantonese, my English and the Mandarin of their new political leadership) to politics and global business. By offering an understanding ear and championing them with corporate HQ, I made a real difference for colleagues I cared deeply about, and thus played my small part in what ultimately was a peaceful, if imperfect, transition. – **Stacie Berdan***

The China Job Market: An Overview

One simple way to see how many China-related jobs are available is to track the Fortune 500 and Global 500 annual lists of America's and the world's largest companies. These mega-firms are increasingly focused on China; a study by China's National Development and Reform Commission (NDRC) found 480 of the Fortune Global 500 had invested in China. I'd love to know how many companies on the US Fortune 500 list are active in China; I suspect most if not all. Much analysis suggests that despite ongoing concerns, given high profitability and surging demand in China, many US firms now invest more there than at home – a trend endorsed by many Wall Street experts. Chinabound US investments appear to be slowing recently, but that may be due more to cash short-flows than desire, since US sovereign debt has been downgraded by Chinese and global ratings agencies.

Looking at the Global 500 rankings, China's rise as investor (job-creator) is clear. Many Chinese firms surged past US counterparts in the 2008 financial crisis. The 2010 list included three Chinese MNCs among the global top 10, and just two from the US; 54 Chinese firms now rank among the Global 500. In fact, foreign direct investment (FDI) into the US by Chinese firms seeking US market share already creates many jobs, despite political restrictions on Chinese FDI that many experts feel harm the US more than they help.

Those big-name multi-national company trends tell just part of the story – in terms of job opportunities probably the smallest part, since small and medium enterprises (SMEs) tend to create more jobs than do large MNCs (according to the US Small Business Administration, 99.7% of all US employers are small firms, which collectively employ more than half of all Americans and generated 64% of all new jobs created in the last 15 years). In today's interconnected world, even the smallest firms benefit from supply chain optimization, niche sales both in the US and overseas, and global cross-fertilization of ideas.

> *As a China business consultant, I once supported primarily large MNCs. Having gone part-time 'mommy track,' I now find helping smaller firms works better for my schedule, and frankly also often feels more meaningful (my daughter is American, and I want her to be able to find a job when she grows up). It's exciting to see how many different US firms, large and small, are thriving and growing and so being able to add jobs there and here based on smart involvement with China.* **–Rebecca Weiner**

Today I am regularly asked for advice from firms of all sizes. Some questions are obvious, like the toy store owner who wanted to directly import Chinese baby toys. Other projects have been pleasant surprises, like helping Optimax, the precision optics manufacturer, with high-tech exports to Shanghai that have brought 50 new manufacturing jobs to Upstate New York. From the medical optics firms I help both import components from and export products to China, to the real estate broker whose investment savvy I help communicate to Chinese investors, smart businesspeople in every field are involving China in their plans. Even while arranging my late mother's funeral I was asked for advice (yes, really) by a funeral director who directly imports low-cost made-in-China caskets.

In other words, in both the US and China, for big firms and small, China-related job opportunities are enormous and growing. In virtually every field, from education to energy, automotive to aerospace, agriculture to zoology, if you have skills or interests and are ready to work, China has opportunities for you.

> *Here at DuPont, I have the opportunity to mentor a lot of our future young leaders, and I tell all of them, study Mandarin, and get on the next plane to Shanghai.* – **Diane Gulyas**

A Bifurcated Market

Those opportunities are not evenly distributed at every level, however. The good news for recent US graduates is that China offers vast entry-level opportunities for native English speakers willing to teach English, copy-edit English documents drafted by Chinese colleagues, conduct English web-research for Chinese firms, and so on.

There are also still top jobs available for experienced managers seen as bringing unique skills. Given how fast China is growing and how challenging the market is – and thus the demands she makes on top managers – there is a shortage of leadership-level executives in China. As a result, much analysis suggests, packages are actually getting fatter these days again for senior executives.

But many mid-level expat jobs are drying up, as MNCs in China work to localize. This is important for companies both to save money (despite rising salaries, most Chinese managers still make less than expats), and to avoid perceived glass ceilings among Chinese staff, who may jump ship if they don't see ample opportunities for promotion.

> *China is increasingly a bifurcated job market for expatriates. China still appreciates, and seeks to emulate, the creative and other benefits of an American education, and values having native English-speakers on the*

*team.... There are plenty of entry-level jobs for young Americans willing to work cheap in return for experience, and there are still senior posts for skilled Western expatriates. But many mid-level expat jobs are disappearing. – **Elizabeth Knup***

Until recently, Knup was one of only a handful of non-Chinese among hundreds of China-based employees of the global education and publishing giant Pearson. Knup points out that having now acquired the Wall Street English schools, which hire only native English speakers as teachers, Pearson today has some 400 expatriate employees among its 3000 employees in China. But again, most of those positions are entry-level teaching jobs.

Remember too that you are competing not just with other would-be expats and with the billion job candidates already in China, but also with the army of globally mobile Chinese "returnees" from work or study abroad, people contemporary slang calls *haigui*, or "sea turtles."

*The subtext in China has changed. Before, expatriates were seen as bringing business to China, helping China grow. Now, we see expats as coming to China to help their careers, as needing China.... So many Chinese have gone abroad...Even we haigui need not just education but experience, something to differentiate us from the fierce competition among top-tier domestic university graduates. – **Michael Zhu***

So given these challenges and the tough competition, if you're thinking seriously about getting involved with China, how can you stand out from the pack of other Americans looking toward Asia as the new "land of opportunity"? Here are 10 Top Tips:

1. **Be ready to work hard**. There's an old joke – not really joking – about 8-hour shifts in China being a half-day. China opportunities aren't as cushy as years ago. Of course, it's important to maintain some life balance; hard work can be overdone. Still, expats do need to pull their weight, and then some.

2. **Don't go crazy with compensation demands.** Once, Americans willing to learn Chinese or work as China expats could command high salaries and perks like cars, drivers and luxury apartments

Those days are long gone except *perhaps* for senior executives. Focus on long-term growth opportunities, not short-term compensation, and you will do just fine.

3. **Focus on what you can bring to China that is different** from what either average Chinese or *haigui* have to offer. This may involve language, life experience or cultural understanding of Western business. Find ways to incorporate your differentiating points into your job-search toolkit. If specific courses or certificates can give you an edge in your chosen field, get them.

4. **Especially focus on skills/abilities in creativity/innovation.** Innovation is a major challenge for China as she seeks to move up the value chain from "made in China" to "created in China" – a complex topic. That means plenty of jobs for consultants who claim to be able to teach creativity, and plenty of openings for Americans in all fields who can bring a creative and innovative approach to the workplace.

5. **Think carefully about what region in China** you want to work in. Television, rail and a growing network of inter-provincial highways are homogenizing China a bit, but her regional variations are still far more pronounced than America's:

    *   China's far north is frigid, her far south jungle-hot and humid, and her far west desert-dry (and some of it very high up). In much of China, people also still spend a lot more of their lives outdoors than is typical in the US, so weather is important.

    *   China's regional cuisines range from searingly spicy to sugar-sweet and garlicky to mild. Where do your tastebuds lead?

    *   Regional language differences are sharp. Everyone under age 60 will speak Mandarin (the official dialect). But many regional people give Mandarin a heavy accent, and talk in dialects like Cantonese or Shanghainese or minority languages like Uighur or Tibetan that are linguistically unrelated to Mandarin.

    *   There's a vast cultural divide between Northern China, near the political capital in Bejing, and Southern China, around the

manufacturing boom towns of Guangzhou and Shenzhen. The Yangtze River Delta Region near Shanghai forms a "buffer zone" between North and South that shares many aspects of both. Are you a trade go-getter? Interested in politics and culture? Want some of each? Decide accordingly.

- Even more enormous economic, political and cultural differences divide China's entire coastal region, north to south, from her rapid-growth inland provincial cities, and again from her vast rural hinterland. Expat positions in China's interior can be tough, as they tend to have the least familiar "creature comforts" and the fewest other expats to chill with – but even as they can be the most challenging, inland positions also often offer top rewards, both financially and in potential for personal and career growth.

- Read widely, starting with articles on regional differences (like between Beijing and Shanghai, or coastal/inland) and then sit with a map and a good tourist guidebook and decide what area will work the best for you and your career.

6. **Learn as much as you can** about China's language, culture and history before you head to China, starting with resources listed.

7. **Strengthen your abilities in cross-cultural communications**, especially your ability to listen, be flexible, maintain an open mind, and be persistent in pursuit of important goals. The resources listed below can help.

8. **Take proper care of the nuts and bolts of relocation**: visa, travel arrangement, shipment, storage, and the rest, as below.

9. **Get in touch with the expat community in China**, before you head over and while you are there. Having some people from your own culture to hang and chill with sometimes can be great prevention for and antidote to homesickness and culture shock.

10. **But don't hang out ONLY with expats**. I am amazed at how many foreigners live in China while spending their days almost entirely with other foreigners, learning little or nothing about

China. These "accidental expats" limit their career potential, harm their companies, and miss out on learning and personal growth.

This list of "hot tips" will help you regardless of which "pathway to China" you follow. Below are some suggestions to get you going.

Pathways to China: The Education Connection

It's a truism that Chinese respect teachers, and focus on education. Despite issues with US schools and Chinese out-testing Americans on math, sciences and even English, Chinese students still love having American teachers. Witness how many Chinese students pour into the US to study. The Institute of International Education estimates that the flow of Chinese students to the US had increased by 80 percent in the last decade. Twenty-three percent of international students in the US are Chinese. Chinese schools also still love hiring Americans – and not just at college level. China's private schools at the elementary and secondary level also typically welcome American teachers.

Why? One word: creativity. China's leaders, recognizing their system's limitations, seek to revamp her educational system to better foster the creativity that drives innovation. And for all its faults, the US education system is seen as a model for fostering creativity. This is the single biggest reason Chinese schools welcome Americans, with or without teacher certification, to teach in China. This is especially true for Americans who teach English; they offer Chinese schools a double bonus – teaching English in ways that also strengthen creativity.

So finding a job as an English teacher of Chinese students has been for decades and still remains the single easiest point of entry to China for Americans. Technically, schools are upgrading requirements. There are "foreign teachers" and "foreign experts"; if possible, you want to be certified as the latter, so you can command a higher salary and benefits. Officially, you need three years of teaching experience and TEFL (Teaching of English as a Foreign Language) certification to qualify as a foreign expert, but many schools will bend or even waive these requirements. Going as a "foreign teacher" can be even easier.

Plan ahead, and you can find a school which will arrange your visa and work permit, pay airfare, and offer you a place to live, a raft of local contact people, and pre-arranged cultural forays throughout your chosen region. Teaching is an excellent way to get paid to get over to China, pay your dues, learn the culture, get grounded in the language, start networking and get ready for an ongoing China-related or global career. I first went to China that way – you can read my aged but still useful recommendations for teachers and students in my book *Living in China*. The actor/director Mark Salzmann took the same route – his experiences led to his lovely book and movie *Iron and Silk*. So did Peter Hessler, who wrote *River Town* and now covers China regularly for *National Geographic*, and many others.

> *Teaching in China is a highly respected job where it's easy to meet people and make friends, while respect for you as a teacher and interest in you as a foreigner helps smooth over your gaffes as you get used to Chinese culture. Levels of censorship and political sensitivity vary greatly, but in general foreign teachers should be more careful about not bringing up sensitive topics than other foreign workers. The good news is, teachers have more free time and more flexible schedules than office workers, so you can make extra money tutoring, or if you prefer, develop a social life. And you get long vacations during which you can travel.* – **Ben Farkas**

It is worth noting that salaries and working conditions (class size, number of classes, working hours, levels of administrative support, teacher training) vary widely between schools. Teaching jobs overall also generally pay less than business jobs, although they are usually locally competitive. Most college or university-level positions for foreign experts are more cushy than elementary or middle school positions for "foreign teachers."

> *I served as a foreign teacher for a year at a middle school post in Hunan Province arranged by a minimal-service sending organization, starting with zero teaching experience or certification. My first time teaching was my first day of class with 70 middle school students and no assistant, where my Chinese was as non-existent as my students' English. This did not stop my sending organization from padding my resume for its own reasons with fake teaching experience and TEFL certification, or from sending me out on*

*'consulting' assignments during what was officially supposed to be my vacation. – **Andrew Howe***

Even within educational levels, jobs vary greatly. Howe's middle school experience involved teaching long hours for low pay while living in Spartan conditions. But others have done very well.

*I taught at a highly respected magnet middle school in relatively wealthy Guangdong province. My students were almost universally attentive, whip-smart and had at least some interest in English, and that made my two years a cakewalk. – **Gus Tate***

*Your best hope is to get in touch with previous teachers at the same institution, since once you take it, you are basically tied to the job for a full year or at least a full semester. – **Ben Farkas***

It is important to think through what each job will require, and how you can best prepare for all aspects of it.

*My early experiences were difficult.... Middle schools in China are a scary place for both teacher and student. Students are held in gated schools from 7:30 AM to 8:15 PM. Classes are rigid, with a heavy focus on repetition. Students are coming of age, but are held under so many rules. In the beginning I was shocked to see my students behaving like angels. Then they realized I wasn't out to get them in trouble, and chose to run as rampant as possible. During my second semester I reeled in the behavioral issues and decided to relax the lessons, which improved the situation dramatically. Nonetheless, until the very last day of teaching, I had students who did not want to give any amount of effort. – **Andrew Howe***

There are many fine resources for finding teaching jobs in China. For English teaching, try the web ads or conferences of TESOL, the national association of Teachers of English to Speakers of Other Languages. There are also many books on teaching in China more recent than mine, like *A Quick Guide to Teaching English in China, The Little Red Book* and *A Manual for Teaching English in China.* Anne Thurston's *Chinabound* remains a staple, and includes information for English teachers and many other types of teaching posts as well.

Many for-profit websites offer China teaching jobs, but do exercise due diligence on all listings. Be sure you understand any fees being charged. Some sites offer pre-departure cultural training and job match-making services for a fee; this may not be a bad investment if you feel unsure you can make those connections and do that research on your own, but check out all your options. Some sites that seem legitimate include Dave's ESL Café, Cathay Teacher, Learn4Good, Maryknoll China Teachers Program and Chinese Culture Center.

For certified teachers and others with advanced degrees, many additional resources are available, from Fulbright fellowships to the PIER organization at Yale (and its equivalents at many other schools) to the Teacher's Exchange Program of the National Committee on US-China Relations and other programs.

One note: while teaching English is a terrific entry-level China job, it is rarely a great career, except for certified teachers taking posts with globally competitive compensation packages at accredited international schools or universities. The entry-level teaching jobs open to virtually any native English speaker can be fun, and they pay enough to support a young person without dependents simply but sustainably in China. But demanding little, they generally also pay little, and offer less in training or advancement. Staying too long in such jobs can be a trap. One meets people in their 40s and 50s who have no real career skills, no savings, and no future other than teaching English at more low-level posts in Asia. You can read some of their funny but sad stories in the book *Unsavory Characters*. Savvy applicants know to treat that first China teaching job as a springboard, not a wallowing pit.

Pathways to China: Job-Seeking Stateside

Want to get right to work in your own field in China, and skip that first job as an English teacher? There are many guides to help you. How many? Well, a recent Google search of "jobs in China for Americans" found some 43 million results. The challenge, as with any Google or other search, is sorting wheat from chaff.

Here is my very personal list of what I consider to be some of the more useful, meaningful China job-related websites out there, starting (as I usually do) with informational articles and with sites sponsored by educational, government and other not-for-profit sources, but also including head-hunters with significant China experience, and some of the better for-profit China job search sites.

<u>Not-for-profit Informational Sites and Articles on Working in China</u>
- US Department of State
- New Zealand Ministry of Foreign Affairs and Trade
- Kiplinger
- Asia Pacific Management Forum
- China Success Stories
- GradPlus.com
- Adam Kornfield's blog site

My favorite serious, sobering and extremely useful article on the good, bad and ugly of a China job search can be found in a recent posting on Forbes blog by Shaun Rein "Should You Look for Work in China?"

<u>Headhunters Active in China</u>
There is an excellent list of headhunters active in China – along with much other useful commentary – on the China Expert site. Some good facts and figures on working in China are available from the executive search firm Hudson Human Relations.

<u>China Job-search Sites</u>
There are literally thousands of these, among the most credible of which are those maintained directly by MNCs listing their own jobs. Choose any firm in your field and search their website for job posts, including "China" as a keyword. Also search the firm's name together with "China." Search and read widely also on your industry in general in China – you will learn useful background, find out who is active and get a good idea who may be hiring.

In addition, many, many for-profit portal websites offer postings of China jobs. Here are a few that seem to have at least a reasonable number of decent job postings from actual employers. There are no guarantees, of course, and due diligence is crucial, but these seem at least not to be total scam sites: Chinajob.com, SimplyHired.com, JobsinChina.com and ChinaXpatJobs.com.

Making Good Use of a China-related Job Search:

Most of the rules for a China job search parallel any job search:

1. Develop your own global job-search toolkit, with a clear but flexible sense of the career path you seek and focus on any background that shows your interest in/aptitude for China jobs.

2. Remember the best jobs are often never posted – if you find in your research a company with a truly good fit, apply to them whether or not they have any posted job openings.

3. Review job postings critically, trying to ensure the job is a good fit for you and the goals you have set out for yourself.

4. Do your due diligence, and research the company both on and off their own website, to make sure the job listing is real and the company one you would want to work for

5. When you do decide to apply for a posting, make sure you tailor your materials to the posting.

For a China job search those rules are doubly important as you think of hopping a plane and heading far from friend and family support. Pay special attention to due diligence, for many posted China jobs have turned out to be outright scams, or to offer working conditions and/or compensation far below that advertised. Some tips:

- Research the company on the web, in the library and via your mentors and networking contacts.

- Ask in discussions with reps and in any interviews about the company's growth plans, and how you can support them. Check their answers (web, library, mentors), and see if they make sense.

- If the employer starts to seem serious about hiring you, ask for and check references from current and previous employees, especially if the employer is one you have not heard of and can find little information about on the web.

- Be cautious with especially "eager" employers, and about heading over quickly. Transfers can happen fast (I once packed up my US life and went to work for BellSouth in Beijing a week after I first talked with them). But be wary about rapid transfers to no-name companies, especially in remote locations.

- Get all compensation promises in writing, ideally in a contract signed before you get on the plane.

- Be especially careful with buying a plane ticket on your own nickel to head for a job with a no-name company in a remote location.

Check everything out before you go. One young American described being sent for what he thought was a short-term teaching assignment, only to find he had been described as an "expert consultant" to clients of the prospective employer, to whom he had been described as a "volunteer." In the end, he found he was not paid for the assignment, which largely involved "being trotted around in meetings so the clients saw there was a white face present."

Above all, use your common sense, and remember the old adage: if it **sounds** too good to be true, it probably **is**.

> *Do you have a China story you'd like to share?*

Pathways to China: Applying to Chinese Companies

More and more Americans today are taking a leap that once would have seemed unimaginable: becoming employees of Chinese firms.

Many jobs with Chinese companies are now advertised in English on international websites. Far more jobs are posted on the most popular Chinese-language job portals. Top among these (the Monster.com of China, for good and bad) is Zhaopin. If you can read Chinese (or are willing to make some guesses based on Google Translate), Zhaopin.com is well-worth checking out.

In many ways, applying to and working for a Chinese company is the same as applying to and working for a US company. You still need your job search toolkit. You still need to tailor your materials for each posting. And you still need to work hard and pay your dues.

Americans working for Chinese companies must also pay special attention to cultural issues. Some differences in business culture that often require adjustment for new American arrivals include:

- Strong concern with "face" among Chinese colleagues and superiors, which requires some finesse in everything from constructive criticism to providing ideas in meetings which include people senior to you.

- Expectations of commitment to and support for the Chinese employer's global expansion plans, even when those plans may affect employment or other factors at home.

- Adapting to expectations of longer working hour and shorter vacation times than you may be used to.

- Requirements for demonstrating respect for Chinese bosses, in a corporate culture that is likely more rigidly hierarchical than what you are used to.

- Cultural norms that may value relationships and long-term team-work over short-term business or personal goals.

- Differences in social and business protocol and etiquette, in everything from handling of seating arrangements to business cards to table manners to gift-giving

- General cross-cultural communications: what we mean by nods, silences, etc.

There are more good pointers and insights on working for Chinese companies at: Knowledge@Wharton, Zest & Zen International, and Wall Street Cheat Sheet

Do be sure that the job you are being offered is real, not just a temp placement so that the Chinese company has a foreigner to roll out for "face" reasons at this or that event.

If you do have a real opportunity with a Chinese firm, it may well be one of the best opportunities you could have. An American-born financier, now a senior executive with one of China's leading insurance firms, put it this way: "Working with the best Chinese firms is an exciting ride and provides access to growth and opportunity that is difficult for foreign firms in China to match." He cautioned that such opportunities don't come easily: "One of three things must be true for a career for a foreign executive within a top Chinese firm to be sustainable and rewarding: 1. You must bring critical technical expertise that the company has a broadly recognized need for, or 2. You can help create access to Western markets in support of expansion plans, and/or 3. You are backed directly from the top to bring in new management practices not easily found in China." The executive preferred not to be named for this book, which by itself says something about the levels of caution in Chinese firms.

In general, be flexible, pleasant and persistent about important goals, and keep your sense of humor about life, the workplace, and yourself, and you may find that working for a Chinese firm becomes or launches a terrific career.

Are you an American who works for a Chinese company?

Pathways to China: Not-for-profit and Government Jobs

When I first went over in the mid-1980s, China still was and thought of itself as poor, and foreigners working for not-for-profit aid and development agencies were among the most respected (and often best-paid) foreigners in China.

Today, with China's economy booming, much has changed; not-for-profit posts are certainly no longer the best paid jobs. Still, many Chinese still have a special fondness and respect for foreigners who come to China in a helping role. For all its newfound wealth, China still faces issues from the environment to epidemics and natural disasters to labor rights and growing rural-urban inequities. Foreigners who are thoughtful and well-informed and working within accepted government-to-government or non-governmental organization (NGO) exchanges are welcomed. If anything, foreigners in NGOs often meet with more welcome and optimism among the Chinese they deal with than they do among other foreigners involved with China.

Government and NGO opportunities require different job searches than do jobs for for-profit companies. The process is often much longer, involving things like background and security checks (for the government posts) and relatively intensive training (for both). The rewards can be great, including a real sense of accomplishment from helping directly tackle some of the pressing problems of the day, as well as deep insight into Chinese and world issues, and a strong network of connections that can help with any later career move.

For government jobs, a good place to start is a fine Bureau of Labor Statistics publication on working abroad which includes of US government agencies with interests overseas, including in China, with details on what each is looking for and how to apply. Follow up with the classic book *Careers in International Affairs*. Your college or university's career advisory office should also have extensive information available on government agencies from the military to the State Department to USAID and beyond, all of whom regularly hire people with China-related skills and interests.

For not-for-profits, it is worth checking with all the major global NGOs discussed in this book in Chapter 6.

In addition, there is an excellent database of international NGOs, large and small, active in China today available from China Development Brief. Mine this database in your areas of interest (geographic and sector-specific), and you will find a variety of organizations to correspond with, learn from, and potentially apply to. Often you may land a post initially as an intern or volunteer, which if you can swing it financially can be a great way to get over to China, get credentialed and start to learn and meet people. NGO interns and volunteers who do well at their unpaid or poorly-paid jobs will often be able to move on to better-paid work, knowing that they have made a difference for others while paying their own dues.

Pathways to China: Going Without a Pre-Arranged Job
The bravest and riskiest, but at times most effective, way to approach a China job search is to simply save money, buy a ticket and board a plane. This once unheard-of route to China is now quite common. Because many interviews work best in person, and because Chinese appreciate the guts it takes for an American to head to Asia with no sure job lined up, very often the gamble pays off.

There's a big "if" though: the gamble usually pays off if and only IF you do your homework well enough before you leave home to know what to do about logistics and visas, where to go in China, whom to talk with after you arrive, and how to come prepared to make a good impression. Some things to do in advance include:

- Think carefully about Visa issues. Many people have come to China on a tourist (L) visa, found work, exited to Hong Kong, gotten a work (Z) visa and re-entered. However, that approach has become more difficult due to stringent new requirements in Hong Kong's visa system. There is good general information on China visas on www.visarite.com. For up-to-date information, check with the Chinese embassy or consulate nearest you and with a good travel agent who specializes in China as you plan your trip.

- Research, research, research your chosen field in your chosen region: what companies or organizations are active, what are they doing, who are their competitors, what keeps them up at night.

- Reach out to potential employers before you go, seeking to line up interviews in advance so you can hit the ground running.

- Pay attention to safety issues, as detailed in Smarttraveller.gov.au from the Australian government.

- Prepare as well as you can by studying language and cultural background on China and on your chosen region in particular.

- Think deeply about what you can contribute, and carefully tailor your job-search toolkit to the companies you plan to apply with.

- If possible, time your arrival to attend a trade show, seminar, or conference in your chosen field.

- If possible, line up people to visit socially while you are there as well – perhaps even someone whose couch you can crash on when you first arrive. A good place to start looking is in one of the many blogs and online discussion forums for expats in China.

Have you moved to China without a job?

Some people plan an initial look-see visit during which they schedule a raft of interviews and hope to come home with an offer they can pack up for. Others do the packing first, and head to China prepared to stay the duration. Either can work, and the difference is really about how much risk-taking you are up for. Prepare well, be flexible, patient, and persevere; you will do fine.

Pathways to China: Transferring an Established Career

By definition, in any job search beyond the entry level, experience counts. Turning your experience into a China career is all about information: researching what the market needs and who is hiring, and getting the right knowledge to the firms about what you can offer.

So do your homework. Subscribe to and read general China info, and also information specific to your industry. If you are serious about a transfer to China, you should know what is happening in your field and who the key players are (Chinese and MNCs), what the main issues are and what is being done to overcome them. With that information, you can craft a highly relevant elevator speech regarding what you can bring to the table. That will in turn both inform and drive your ongoing career search.

There are three main ways to transferring an established career to China: internal transfers within your current employer, lateral transfers to other firms and starting your own business (discussed more below).

Internal transfers to expat positions in China with fully-loaded compensation packages are getting rarer, and come with more stringent requirements. But fully-loaded transfers do still happen. If you want one, be sure to put your hat in the ring:

- Let everyone you deal with know that you are interested in an international assignment.
- Volunteer for those extra projects, especially ones with an international component.
- Be the person who gets up early or stays up late to join a conference call across time zones.
- Scour the company's website for global listings.
- Ask for and read all research and reports coming out of your company's China operations.
- Reach out to and stay connected with executives currently working for your company or its affiliates in China.
- Understand what issues your company faces in China, and start to formulate creative solutions.
- Study Chinese, using the resources listed below, and otherwise prepare for life in China [hotlink to list below].
- Read widely about global careers, and learn from the tips and advice and models of others. A great place to start is Stacie Berdan's first book, *Get Ahead By Going Abroad*.

Lateral Transfers to Other Firms
These often happen in much the same way as internal transfers, via networking. If you aren't getting where you want to go via an internal transfer, start casting the net wider:

- Let professional associates you deal with in affiliate companies, suppliers, vendors, customers and even competitors know that you are interested in a China post.
- Attend China-related events at business associations in your area and industry, hone your pitch, and network, network, network.

- Consider joining the US-China Business Council (still the premier networking, research, and informational industry association for US businesses active in China). Corporate memberships can be expensive, but individual memberships are under $1000/year.
- Consider reaching out to reputable headhunters such as those listed on China Expert's site.

Typically, people with established careers are also established in other areas of their lives, such as family. If that's true of you, think carefully how any transfer will impact your family as well.

Pathways to China: From First China Job to China Career

However you get to China, whatever first job you land, your first priorities will be to settle in and figure out what the job takes, bring yourself up to speed, and make sure you are meeting or exceeding expectations in the post. As soon as you are doing that, you should start thinking about what comes next.

Much of this is the same in China as anywhere else: paying your dues, doing good work, keeping eyes open and ears to the ground, and relentless networking as described elsewhere in *Go Global*.

In China, networking is even more important than in the US, and in fact is central to advancing your career in China, because:

- Chinese traditionally rely on *guanxi* (relationships) for many business and personal connections, and prefer personal introductions. This stems in part from a cultural norm in which people who give references are somewhat responsible for future behavior by people whom they have recommended – which also explains why Chinese people tend not to give references lightly.
- *Guanxi* is not nearly as central as it once was – relationships alone won't get you much of anywhere in China these days, without also proving you can do the work. But *guanxi* helps ease the way. Relationships alone won't win any races, but they can get you to the right track, on time, with a fair chance at the starting line.

- As more firms localize, and more senior managers are Chinese, Chinese cultural norms around relationships are increasingly important for expat employees. Foreigners who have spent a long time in China also often rely on *guanxi*.

- *Guanxi* networks are both a hurdle to newcomers who have not yet hooked into them, and a major boost for you once you have.

The good news is, building *guanxi* involves largely the same tools you are already familiar with from networking at home – doing good work, getting noticed, attending business meals and events, providing information and insights, exchanging business cards and ideas. Networking tends to be a little more personal in China than in the US, often involving token personal gifts (such as moon-cakes for the Mid-Autumn festival) and non-business time spent together at karaoke or bowling or the like. But those differences pale compared to the similarities with what you are already familiar with. Basically:

- Do your job

- Deliver on your promises

- Be polite and helpful to all you work and deal with

- Ensure management knows you are doing good work without ever being pushy or appearing like a braggart

- Reach out to others in the business community whenever you have an opportunity.

Easy to say and harder to do, of course, but do these things, and you too will be well on your way to building your own *guanxi* network.

Networking with the home office is also crucial. This is important for maintaining connections at home to prepare for home re-entry after expat postings, a topic explored in *Get Ahead By Going Abroad*. Equally, networking with the home office lets you become a go-to "China expert" for the home team, while helping the China team communicate effectively with HQ. Bridging between the languages, cultures, working styles, and concerns of HQ and China operations is the single most powerful role an expat can play.

The reason for this, the truth that so many expats miss is this: you will NEVER be the "China expert" that your Chinese colleagues are. The lowliest "office boy" or "cleaning girl" who grew up in China knows more about China and Chinese culture than you will ever learn. Your goal is not to try to outlearn your Chinese colleagues about China, but to mentor them in communicating their knowledge in ways that make business sense to western audiences. By earning the trust and respect of your Chinese colleagues and helping them communicate, you can help unlock their insights and analysis. This will strengthen the business you all serve, and all of your careers.

Social networking is also growing in China, where the world of bloggers is exploding. Some experts believe Chinese-language web content will soon outpace English content by volume. Today, social networking in China is widely seen as more useful for product marketing than job-searching; when researchers write about social networking and jobs in China, they mean the old-fashioned social networking that happens via clubs and neighborhood associations. But as today's web-savvy teens become tomorrow's executives, digital social networking is likely to grow in very quickly. Certainly, in China as in the US, it is already crucial to monitor your and your employer's online brands, and be wary of posting extreme or compromising materials that could get you denied a job down the line.

For now, the old-fashioned fundamentals still apply in China. In sum: be trustworthy, and gain the trust of your Chinese colleagues based on your knowledge, hard work, dedication to the job, and sincere concern for them as colleagues and human beings. Your advancement in China will grow primarily out of that.

Pathways to China: Starting A Business in China

Starting your own business in China may seem daunting, and probably should not be the first thing you do there. But many, many people from around the world have successfully gone this route, setting their own terms for how they want to operate.

There are still many opportunities for ambitious individuals in China. The economy is growing and the market large enough that countless niches remain to be filled. Wages are also still many times lower than in the West, so services and products can be developed and offered with lower investment. Just be aware that the wealth of opportunities is in direct proportion to the difficulties. China has never been easy and her regulatory complexities are growing as fast as her economy. Most importantly, small no-name start-ups have difficulty convincing good staff to work for them. Most successful start-ups strike partnerships with young, ambitious Chinese, joining capabilities from both worlds. Trading is another easy way to start, in high-tech or high-quality niche products where both knowledge of the field and connections abroad will provide strong advantages against would-be copycats. – **Nicholas Musy**

The opportunities are not evenly distributed throughout China; new arrivals should think beyond the already-developed coast.

One model for entrepreneurs unafraid to be pioneers is to check what has worked in Hong-Kong, Shanghai and Beijing and bring it to booming second and third tier cities, which in many ways are 10 years behind the coast. Chongqing on the Yangtze river 2500 kilomteres west of Shanghai, for example, is one of the largest cities in the world with 30 million inhabitants, and growing fast. Wuhan, the geographical center of China, is now within 3.5 hours high speed train of Beijing, Shanghai and Guangzhou. There are many other boom-towns. By contrast, those who insist on enjoying the convenience of the developed East will increasingly need to bring specialized knowledge which gives an edge over the locals, who have become very savvy entrepreneurs as well! – **Nicholas Musy**

There is an excellent blog on ForeignEntrepreneursinChina.com and another on DoingBusiness.org. And of course, there are libraries full of books, magazines, e-newsletters, conference reports, and other resources on doing business in China as noted below

The bottom line for starting any business has to be the fire in your belly the willingness to do what it takes to make a new business work. Only you can answer whether or not you have that. Just remember, whatever stick-to-it-iveness you would need to start a business in America, you will probably need multiples of to make a new business work in China. But given relative rates of economic growth, the rewards can also be correspondingly greater.

Preparing Before You Go

China is simultaneously one of the most and least foreign cultures Americans may ever get involved with. Trade patterns make made-in-China goods familiar all over the world, while the historic Diaspora of Chinese people means virtually everyone knows and likes sweet-and-sour and stir-fry. More and more Chinese speak English, have travelled or lived abroad and understand global standard practices. Yet China remains linguistically, culturally, geographically and politically very much its own world.

You almost can't over-prepare for entering and working in that world. Not all China hands agree with this of course; I have a friend who advises against reading too many books on China before going, for fear of arriving with too many preconceived notions. But even he admits that in many, many areas, forewarned is forearmed.

Americans often experience particularly strong culture shock in China, a country poles apart from ours in politics, culture, parenting, business ethics and other areas. I was no different. My first months in Hong Kong were difficult in many ways. But in time I adapted, with help from my Hong Kong colleagues. You can too. – **Stacie Berdan**

Three areas where pre-departure preparation can be especially helpful include language, culture/history and cross-cultural communications.

Language

Chinese is widely seen as an especially difficult language for non-native speakers, but in my experience that is true only of China's complicated written characters. Spoken Chinese uses simple, logical grammar rules that make it in some ways quite easy. Still, it's a high enough wall that even today, remarkably few non-Chinese people living and working in China learn Chinese. Imagine Chinese people trying to land senior executive positions in the US without speaking English and you'll see how ridiculous that is.

Even a little survival Chinese will help, and the more you learn, the better. Ability to fluently conduct business in Chinese is a high standard, and definitely not necessary to succeed. Many foreigners who DO speak fluent Chinese choose to conduct business in English for positioning reasons, or for the benefit of others around the table, or to get extra time to think during interpretation. But from the all-important perspectives of "face" and *guanxi*-building, learning some Chinese is well-worth the effort.

Here are some tips on formal language-learning programs:

- If you are still a student, seek out your school's Chinese courses.

- If not, consider part-time classes at a community college or similar, or an intensive summer course. As Chinese has emerged as a popular new language for Americans, thousands of Chinese schools and study programs have popped up, of varying quality.

- Perhaps the premier program in the US remains the Middlebury-Monterey Language Academy, whose intensive summer courses have trained generations of diplomats and business leaders.

- There are also many excellent language programs in China, such as those listed on LexioPhiles and in my book *Living in China.*

- Alternately, programs local to you may be convenient and affordable while also offering excellent quality. Get recommendations from others in your area as to the quality.

- Many of the best programs are taught by accredited teachers who are members of the Chinese Language Teachers Association.

There are many programs now available to students at high school and even elementary school, either term-time or during summer vacation. There are also more and more students taking gap years between high school and college to study Chinese. There are also fine self-study and on-line options. Some not-for-profit sites worth looking at, many put together at least initially by dedicated volunteers:

- PinYin.info

- MandarinTools.com

- LearningChineseOnline.net
- ChinaLinks
- AsiaSociety.org
- ChineseOutpost.com
- Chinese-forums.com has an excellent list compiled by the wonderfully dedicated editors there of the best of the thousands of Chinese language study materials out there, including both free and for-profit products.

Self-study can work best when combined with tutoring or language exchange. Reach out to native Chinese speakers living in your area via postings on websites and/or bulletin boards at colleges or universities in your area, or even via Craigslist. People you contact can put you in touch with community groups and social associations which will also help you learn more about China's culture, history, and politics. Just remember that the Chinese Diaspora community living in America has its own culture and politics which are often distinct from (though colored by) the culture and politics of China.

Culture/History

It can be hard to know where to start seeking to understand the history and culture of a country of 1.3 billion people that revels in a 5000-year tradition (however questionable the claim of "unbroken" history may be). But you have to start somewhere. And the more you know, the better you will be able to function in China, where culture and history – and frequent reinterpretations of history – color everything.

Here to get you started is a recommended list of my favorite "recommended lists" for books, movies, and other resources on Chinese culture and history:

- The *Asia for Educators* database is excellent and searchable by geographic region, time period, and subtopic.
- Stanford's SPICE initiative on global education has many terrific materials available through the Road to Beijing link.

- The China threads on TheBrowswer.com are well worth following.
- The five best books on China list from ChinaLawblog.com includes several of my favorites. Ditto the five best Chinese films list for films at Cayman Financial Review.

And here are a few older books and films I love to recommend:

- *Sharks Fins and Millet,* by Illona Ralf Sues and *Stillwell and the American Experience in China* by Barbara Tuchman, for understanding how the Chinese Communist Party (CCP) came to power, and why they were – and are – so supported by so many in China despite their many disastrous meanders.
- *When Red is Black* by Qiu Xiaolong and *Life and Death in Shanghai* by Nien Cheng to understand some of the CCP's worst meanders.
- *China Men* by Maxine Hong Kingston and the film *Wedding Banquet,* directed by Ang Lee, to understand the importance of family in Chinese culture.
- Lu Xun's great story *Kong Yi Ji,* and the Hugh Dean book *Good Deeds and Gunboats,* to understand why so many in China still blame the West for China's "period of humiliation," and the film *Hero,* directed by Zhang Yimou, to understand China's sense of its own once and future greatness.

Culture Shock and Cross-cultural Communications

In addition to learning as much as you can about China's language, culture and history, it is also worth spending time thinking about, planning for, and preparing against culture shock, and strengthening your abilities in cross-cultural communications.

Much of this is the same for China as it is for any other country. Review the sections in Chapter 2 on culture shock and cross-cultural communications to familiarize yourself with the topic.

But in this as in so many other areas, China also has idiosyncrasies worth being aware of. For a negative review of Chinese culture, written in the guise of advice about culture shock by a writer who appears to be suffering from culture shock (although he is in fact Chinese), see the book *Posted to China: Find Out What Corporate HR Did Not Tell You,* by Ken Zhong. For a more thoughtful, though also unvarnished, discussion of some of China's less appealing cultural values written by a true insider, see Bo Yang's famous (and in China, famously banned) book *The Ugly Chinaman.* There are of course real negatives in Chinese as in any culture: think about how foreigners first arriving in the U.S. view our epidemics of obesity, waste, debt, political follies and tendencies toward triumphalism. You should consider in advance, early, and often how you will deal with and adjust to China's issues as well as her many wonderful aspects. For some good advice, hints, tips and tricks on adjusting, see the posts on culture shock at MiddleKingdomLife.com and AmityFoundation.org.

Closely related to the question of culture shock is that of cross-cultural communications, and again in addition to general reading on the topic, I recommend China-specific information. Fortunately, there are many excellent resources. Some good places to start include the articles on cross-cultural communications in China by Yu Qiuyu on Danwei.org and by Bryce Roberts on eChinacities.com, as well as a Geert Hofstade analysis of Chinese communications styles on cyborlink.com, an analysis on US and Chinese communication styles on 1000ventures.com, and a summary of Chinese language and communications at Kwintessential.co.uk. Some useful books include Scott Seligman's *Chinese Business Etiquette,* Charles Lee's *Cowboys and Dragons,* and *Eastern and Western Daily Life: Intercultural Communication in China,* by Robert Smith, Jeanette Lochner and Linda Lei.

Nuts and Bolts of Living and Working in China

As with any transfer overseas, there are many practical considerations, including visas, vaccine, accommodation, and shipping requirements, as well as travel arrangements. As these topics are covered in great detail on the sites of many fine service firms, I will not try to recreate the wheel here, but instead refer readers as follows:

Senior people relocating to or from China with significant shipments of property will want to use a professional relocation service, especially if you will be moving with pets. Several offer substantial useful relocation information on shipments, accommodations, vaccines and other nuts and bolts free on their websites, such as MoveOneInc.com and Second Chance Animal Aid. I have had good experiences working with Crown Worldwide for relocation, and they used to have some of the best free China relocation info available anywhere on their website. They have taken down open access to it, but presumably will still grant it if you register with them for a quote on their services.

If you are going on your own with just a few bags, you will likely not need or be able to afford a full-service relocation company. However you will must pay close attention to relocation procedures. There are good tips for shipping on your own on EasyExpat.com.

For basic visa procedures, see the official China site at www.china-embassy.org, or ChinaSmith's travel agent site (that's the travel agent I use whenever I need support for my own China travels, and I highly recommend them –I have not solicited or received compensation for this endorsement). There is good insight on work visas at Klako Group's site as well. Be sure you dot i's and cross t's on your visa, or you may find yourself deported (if you can get to China in the first place). Also pay attention to the limits on your visa; do not overstay! For up-to-date China health and vaccine information see the CDC and World Health Organization websites.

For China travel information, there are almost too many resources available to recommend any, but here are a few that stand out: The US Department of State offers many China travel information resources. ChinaSmith truly is an outstanding China travel agency. The *Lonely Planet* people continue to offer great budget China travel info (bias alert – years ago I wrote for them). Academic Travel Abroad is my favorite place to refer more well-heeled travelers for China itineraries with real depth as well as luxury – all their tours include an academic lecturer (bias alert – years ago I was one of their tour assistants).

Resources

If I say so myself, I believe you will find useful insights in the following books I have co-authored or contributed chapters to:

- *The New Culture Shock! China*
- *Culture Shock! Shanghai*
- *Living in China*
- *Chinese Intellectual Property Law and Practice* (chapter on communications and IPR)
- *Handbook of Popular Chinese Culture* (chapter on Lifestyles)

Once you are on the ground in China you will find many resources to keep you informed. Here are a few of my favorites to get you started.

General China Resources

In addition to preparing via the reading and viewing lists above, for current information, visit the websites of the National Committee on US China Relations, the Asia Society, the China Society, the China Institute. Read widely on websites such as Danwei.org, SCMP.com and Asia.WSJ.com. And for a portal to the official Chinese government media – which is very useful to read for understanding the government's perspective – ChinaToday.com

Business-Specific Resources

The US-China Business Council and the US-China Chamber of Commerce and the American Chamber of Commerce of China (and its sub-chambers in Beijing, Shanghai, Guangzhou and elsewhere) are great places to get started.

There are libraries full of books, magazines, e-newsletters, reports and other resources on China business. The US-China Business Council's *China Business Review* is a great resource. Another is a list of top-10 recommended books on China for businesspeople, put together by Dan Harris[3], lawyer and author of the excellent China Law Blog, itself an excellent read. Harris maintains an excellent list of other China business blogs, so thorough and thoughtful that I have little to add. In addition to the books Harris lists, I do highly recommend the following, all by friends, and all books I consider must-reads:

- Sheila Melvin's *Little Red Book of China Business*
- Ted Plafker's *Doing Business in China*
- Scott Seligman's *China Business Etiquette*

Expatriate Community Resources

The following are websites dedicated not to Chinese culture, but to the particular culture of the expatriate community in China. They will help you relatively little in understanding China, but they can be great resources for connecting with other expats and having fun while you are there:

- LostLaoWai.com
- BeijingScene.com
- CityWeekend.com
- ThatsShanghai
- Internations

There are literally thousands of other blogs, websites, forums, portals and chat groups dedicated to China and living and working in China. You will quickly find your own favorites. Good luck and enjoy!

---

[3] http://www.forbes.com/2009/12/21/china-business-global-economy-opinions-contributors-daniel-p-harris.html

Top Tips on Navigating the Pathways to China

- Get ready to work hard.

- Learn as much as you can about China.

- Learn or practice the language.

- Focus on what you can bring to China that is different.

- Focus on your skills and abilities in creativity and innovation.

- Be realistic about compensation.

- Consider which region in China you want to work in.

- Strengthen your abilities in cross-cultural communications.

- Take proper care in steps for relocation.

- Network with the expat community in China.

- Make local friends and soak up the culture.

- Take time to relax, de-stress and enjoy yourself!

Go Global!

CPSIA information can be obtained at www.ICGtesting.com
Printed in the USA
LVOW11s2132050814

397735LV00002B/191/P

9 780983 943914